658.311.1

957

D1587637

IRISH LIBRARY INSTITUTE

19 JUL 2013

Using
PSYCHOMETRICS

A Practical Guide to Testing and Assessment

Robert Edenborough

KOGAN
PAGE

First published in 1994

The masculine pronoun has been used throughout this book. This stems from a desire to avoid ugly and cumbersome language, and no discrimination, prejudice or bias is intended.

Apart from any fair dealing for the purposes of research or private study, or criticism or review, as permitted under the Copyright, Designs and Patents Act, 1988, this publication may only be reproduced, stored or transmitted, in any form or by any means, with the prior permission in writing of the publishers, or in the case of reprographic reproduction in accordance with the terms of licences issued by the Copyright Licensing Agency. Enquiries concerning reproduction outside those terms should be sent to the publishers at the undermentioned address:

Kogan Page Limited
120 Pentonville Road
London N1 9JN

© Robert Edenborough, 1994

British Library Cataloguing in Publication Data
A CIP record for this book is available from the British Library.

ISBN 0 7494 1302 6

Typeset by BookEns Ltd, Baldock, Herts.
Printed and bound in Great Britain by Clays Ltd, St Ives plc

Contents

DEDICATION

To Tom, James and Marion,
sources of inspiration in all my endeavours.

List of Figures

Preface

Some years ago I found myself on a plane bound for Scotland with a box containing the *Wechsler Adult Intelligence Scale* in my luggage, *en route* to my first professional application of a psychometric instrument. I was pleased at having the opportunity of exercising the skills I hoped I had learnt on my first degree course, but that I had not been called upon to demonstrate previously. The assignment was a rather atypical one. I was due to make assessments on a range of staff working in the specialised field of air traffic control simulation. These people had already been recruited but were to be assigned to a variety of different tasks to create as realistic an environment as possible for a range of new air traffic control procedures to be evaluated. A number of them were to play the role of pilots who would be in simulated radio contact with a group of real controllers who would form the other human elements in the system. The test was being used to help slot the role players into the pilot and other roles required in the simulation.

Since then I have undertaken a wide range of applications of psychometrics. Many of them have been within the mainstream of testing, such as large scale graduate recruitment, outplacement counselling, and the design and execution of development centres for information technology project managers. Other applications have been less commonplace as in reviewing the work of colleagues who had developed a trainability test for dental technicians or seeking to find an off-the-shelf paper and pencil instrument for measuring manual dexterity in space station personnel. Along the way I have also had the opportunity to take part in original research, and to review and discuss the research of others.

Very often I have found myself asked to explain what is meant by psychometrics or why tests do work, or equally, don't work, how it is that people can't just always cheat when doing personality questionnaires, not to mention why I sometimes refuse to deliver the goods to the manager who sends an assistant to phone me up and ask for 'the tests'. Sometimes the answers that I have given to such questions and enquiries have actually taken me into the preparation of lectures or inputs to in-company courses on assessment matters. What I have always tried to convey in such cases is that although sometimes the technology may be complex, the principles behind testing are relatively simple. Essentially one is seeking to use systematic methods to find out about systematic patterns in the behaviour of other people.

It was, in fact, on the basis of some of these lectures and the discussions that often preceded them that the germ of an idea for a book arose. There are, of course, many books on psychometrics and associated matters already, but it was the notion of use of psychometrics rather than any general theoretical or statistical exposition that seemed to me to provide a worthwhile set of messages. It is this book, then, that is intended to convey those messages.

I have avoided theory and statistics as far as possible, albeit using the device of technical notes where I thought there was value in expanding upon a slightly more arcane idea. The aim has been to produce a book for the intending or perhaps the novice user rather than the specialist.

I have referred to a number of tests, but not a very large number. A simple listing, for instance, of the most commonly used personality questionnaires in print does not seem to be particularly helpful and struck me as potentially more apparently evaluative than I would have intended. The reader is referred to Appendix 2, though, where a list of test publishers is given. Their catalogues, training and other guidance will amply fill the requirements of anyone seeking to get to grips with particular types of instrument.

Although psychometric tests as such form the main matter of this book, I have undertaken a substantial excursion in one chapter into the area of associated techniques and methods ranging from assessment centres to content analytic procedures. Some of these are actually rather a long way removed from the general run of psychometric tests, but others can be regarded as quite near neighbours. In fact as many organisations will draw upon these methods as well as from the more familiar paper and pencil tests it seemed important to me for the intending user to have some feel for the interplay among this whole psychometric neighbourhood.

I have used case studies and examples throughout the text, and hope these will clarify points made and help them to be remembered more easily. As the reader will gather these case studies are drawn in varying degrees from real life. What I have identified as true stories have had personal and other details altered and have sometimes been transposed from their original industries and settings. The more apparently fictional cases are, in fact, blendings of different real situations experienced by myself or colleagues over the years. Throughout I have endeavoured to emphasise the need for and value of taking an integrated approach to the use of psychometrics, and it is largely for this reason that there is substantial cross-referencing among the different chapters.

Fundamentally, psychometric instruments are practical management tools. Their use does, of course, require specialised training but also requires some practical thought involving the posing and answering of why, how, what, who, when and where questions. This book is intended to supply some of the answers.

R A Edenborough
Esher
May 1994

Acknowledgements

Many colleagues in MSL have assisted in the development of this book. I should, though, point out that the ideas expressed are my own and should not be taken as necessarily representing the views or policy of MSL Group International Limited, or any of its subsidiary companies. Bertie Maxwell suggested that I should write the book, so fanning the spark of the idea. Barry Cushway and Derek Lodge added their breath to the flames – and told me it wouldn't be too much trouble – which in retrospect has been true. Kiki Peros and Lynn Shaw helped with the necessary correspondence, and Sheelagh McCrea has been encouraging throughout. Andrew Harley supplied the consultant's report material, and Roy Hammond reviewed and gave helpful comments on the chapter on regulation. Nigel Bastow of MSL Advertising willingly agreed to help with the figures, and their genesis was assisted by Ian White, Ben Wheeler and Bob Randall, while Lyndon Austin undertook their actualisation. Doug Prior supplied ideas, support, original material and helpful comments throughout, finally reviewing and commenting on the entire text.

Barbara Phillips has coped cheerfully, promptly and accurately with an at times arachnoid manuscript, admitting of no problems and eagerly exploring the boundaries of her wordprocessor. My sons, Tom and James, have regarded the whole venture most positively and have provided insightful comment on selected passages. My wife, Marion, has not only coped with my near total non-involvement in domestic duties – down from an already low level – but has advised in detail on content, reading and rereading successive drafts.

I should also like to thank the many business clients who have enriched my experience of psychometrics. Finally I should like to express my gratitude to the many thousands of individuals who have undertaken psychometric procedures with me, as recruitment, counselling or development candidates, or as research subjects.

Nay, answer me. Stand and unfold yourself.

Hamlet, I, i

1

Psychometrics – setting the scene

MENTAL MEASUREMENT AND MAGIC

Tests in action

A small group use sewing machines, working at stitching two squares of material together to make a pocket shape. A manager sits at a computer terminal, tapping in responses to a series of personality questions. A middle-aged woman completes a series of questions about her preferences for different types of work activity. Sixty students, all due to graduate in a few months' time, are arrayed in a hotel conference suite which is set out like an examination hall. Under the watchful eyes of a group of administrators they solve problems in verbal reasoning. A scientist studies a long series of numbers and then tries to reproduce them in reverse order.

All of these people are undertaking psychometric tests. Psychometrics literally means mental measurement and psychometric tests or instruments are measurement devices. The measurement is used to gain understanding of an individual so as to be able to predict behaviour and provide a basis for future action.

Stitching the square of material neatly and accurately will be seen as evidence of ability to train as a machinist in the garment industry. A consultant will write a report on the manager, advising a client as to whether he will fit in with a management team. The middle-aged woman will spend time with a counsellor who will use her responses to help guide her decisions about a change of career. Some of the students will be invited on to another stage of selection and a few will be asked to join the graduate programme of a major multi-national. If the scientist can repeat the numbers accurately and if she performs well on a variety of other tasks she will be selected for work conducting experiments in space.

Thus the applications of psychometrics are various and the benefits arising from their use can include the following:

- Maximising an organisation's performance by improving accuracy of selection.
- Improving employee retention by better matching individuals to jobs.
- Avoiding the financial and personal costs associated, on both sides, with poor recruitment decisions.
- Optimising the use of people's capacities by helping focus development activity.
- Achieving better career management by matching individual aspirations to organisations' opportunities.

In fact many people have found psychometric tests to be of very substantial value, but practices in test use are still patchy, variable and often idiosyncratic. In this book a number of aspects of psychometric testing are considered, to help readers see these powerful tools in a broad perspective. The context in which tests are used is in essence the very broad one of understanding and predicting behaviour. As such they interplay with a range of other systematic and less systematic methods. The latter, of course, include the broad sweep of intuitive and largely unconscious devices that we all use in making sense of our fellow beings. The warm smile, the educational background, the manner of speech, the real or supposed slight, arriving five minutes early or five minutes late, all give us day-to-day clues from which we build pictures of friends, colleagues, acquaintances or strangers and which we seek to use to come to conclusions about their enduring behavioural characteristics. The fact that psychometric tests do much the same thing, but through the medium of ritualised questioning and the manipulation of symbols places them among the black arts in the minds of some. But they are not magical, they are, rather, scientific distillations of much practical, intuitive experience, contained in the convenient form of standardised sets of items.

The main focus of this book, then, will be upon assisting managers, personnel professionals and others to have a practical appreciation of the ways in which psychometric tests and associated instruments may be of use to them in their work, perhaps to dispel some of the more mystical associations without destroying the potency of these valuable devices.

Plan of the book

This chapter and the succeeding one set the scene, with some historical comment, definitions and key concepts. Chapters 3, 4 and 5 look at the main types of application likely to be important to managers, namely selection and development. The ideas explored in those chapters are returned to in a practical sense in Chapter 8 which is designed as a guide to working with one's own application of psychometrics. The intervening Chapters, 6 and 7, make important excursions to underpin practical use. Chapter 6 looks at the range of regulatory considerations that need to be taken into account in any effective and professionally based use of psychometric tests. Chapter 7 looks at a variety of other procedures often used in conjunction with psychometric tests and which have some elements of similarity to what are normally regarded as psychometric methods. These range from interview procedures with varying degrees of structure to methods involving direct work sampling techniques.

The concluding chapter comments on the role of the user of tests and looks ahead at the emerging future for psychometrics. A glossary is provided and comments and technical notes are appended in Appendix 1, as are details of test publishers in Appendix 2.

HISTORICAL PERSPECTIVE

Early days

Psychometric tests have a history which, although not long, goes back further than is often realised. They originated in work related to education in the latter part of the nineteenth century, for example by the American Cattell (1890), and the Frenchmen Binet and Henri (1895), with the first published test being produced by Binet and another associate Simon in 1905. They were taken up subsequently in a number of select fields.

Notable among these was the work for the American Armed Forces during the First World War (Yoakum and Yerkes 1920). Here it was important to identify the abilities of very large numbers of young men quickly, so as to channel them into the most suitable military roles and the most appropriate training. Part of the early scientific interest surrounding tests centred on the way in which intelligence could be described and its structure characterised. There was debate, for instance, on the number of factors into which general intelligence could be divided (eg Spearman 1904).

The general way in which tests should be applied was set out fairly early on in this process, with scientific and professional standards being progressively laid down. For example the National Institute of Industrial Psychology (NIIP) in Britain began formally teaching test use and administration in the 1920s. The American Psychological Association (APA) first issued standards for testing in the very early days (1905 as reported by Cronbach 1964) with progressive development subsequently (APA 1954, APA et al 1974).

Tests were found to be useful because they contributed to the prediction and understanding of behaviour. As such they owed much to another tradition in psychology, that of the experimentalists, in which observations of behaviour were made under controlled and standardised laboratory conditions.

The physician and physicist Fechner working in the mid nineteenth century first brought quantitative methods into the field of human experience. He sought mathematical relationships linking physical stimuli - light, heat - to their effects in the intensity of sensations experienced. In 1879 Wundt, sometimes described as the father of experimental psychology, founded a laboratory at Leipzig, devoted to the application of scientific method to behaviour and sensory experience. Among the disciplines contributed by these laboratory based approaches were those of standardisation of procedures. These included the same stimuli applied under the same conditions, with set instructions, recording of responses and common methods of interpretation.

The Second World War and onward

In the UK and the US in particular, development of a number of tests for specific military roles and trades took place during the

Second World War. Testing for particular types of civilian occupation had started to be developed in the inter-war period (eg Burt 1922, Spielman 1923) and this trend continued after the Second World War, with developments such as the publication of the Differential Aptitude Tests (DAT) in the US (Bennett et al 1947). This was designed to aid occupational guidance and, as such, could be useful to employers and potential employees. It comprised a battery of tests, covering a number of areas from abstract reasoning and abstract spatial relationships to the solution of mechanical problems and spelling.

Small group testing for guidance became more common at this time, whereas prior to the Second World War the more labour intensive individual testing had been usual. In the UK at the same time test development research in the occupational field continued to be undertaken in particular by the National Institute for Industrial Psychology (eg Castle and Garforth, 1951, Vincent 1955, Stott 1956). Since then there has been a continued growth of the development and application of testing.

The second edition of Anastasi's book on testing, published as far back as 1961, lists nearly 1200 references to research on published tests. Since 1941 large numbers of tests have been catalogued and reviewed in the *Mental Measurement Year-books*, originally edited by Buros. This enormous output has progressively found its way into commercial and organisational use. In the UK some large scale employers such as British Telecom (BT) have had their own specialist testing departments for many years, developing and applying testing procedures quite broadly.

Back from the present

A current British Psychological Society (BPS) 'flyer' cites a 1989 survey indicating use of occupational tests among 73 per cent of major UK companies. Williams (1994) reviewing test use as indicated by a number of surveys sees a picture of increasing test use. Yet testing has never been anything like universal and has been variable in its application. For example, Bevan and Fryatt (1988) reported much higher evidence of test use in connection with managerial, technical and professional staff, than for manual workers and their foremen and supervisors. The present author, while exploring the use of psychometrics among law firms, found reactions ranging from suspicion and amazement that such steps should be contemplated to their application as a matter of routine.

To make what may seem an extreme comparison, despite widespread use psychometric testing has never achieved the currency as a systematic way of looking at people that, say, standard accounting practices have gained for examining the figures and trends within a business.

A number of reasons for this state of affairs present themselves. To begin with many tests have been developed on the basis first of psychological theory and only second in relation to practical applications. This has meant that interpretation has required comprehension of theoretical ideas and material beyond the layperson. The widespread development of training courses in test use for people other than specialists has been a relatively recent phenomenon, going hand in hand with growth in the number of test publishers and distributors. (The 1966 edition of Cronbach's *Essentials of Psychological Testing* listed 18 leading test publishers and distributors in the US; nearly as many can be found today serving the much smaller UK market.)

Also, despite the strong academic threads and the evident need for detailed understanding, formal controls on test use have been of relatively late date. For example, at the time of writing, the BPS is still deliberating standards of competence necessary to govern individuals choosing and interpreting personality questionnaires. Thus poor practices were able to grow up in some areas with tests tending to be subject to a variety of misuses. Although there have, thankfully, been few major scandals, tests became associated in the minds of some with casual rather than professional practices.

There was a spate of litigation in the US in the 1970s, following the equal employment legislation of the 1960s. This led to extreme wariness on the part of some employers and their dropping of the use of tests. The parent company of at least one American test publisher withdrew entirely from that business at that time. In the UK, cases such as that of a group of ethnic minority British Rail employees, who successfully contested the use of particular test procedures (Kellett et al 1994) have arisen from time to time.

It is also evident that tests used in occupational settings to aid recruitment and selection decisions will often give different indications from those provided by conventional, biographically based, interviews. Thus there can be an element of competition between psychometric testing procedures and methods very dear to the intuitive heart of many managers!

Clearly there have been boosts to test use, too. One of the most recent has been the competency movement – which is providing a common language – albeit an imperfectly understood one, with its links to initiatives such as the National Vocational Qualifications (NVQs) in the UK. So today, following a chequered history, psychometric tests are extensively but by no means universally in use. Similarly, understanding of their value and potential is widespread, but still patchy. Their roots and progress are summarised below.

A FEW MILESTONES IN THE HISTORY OF PSYCHOMETRIC TESTING

- 1879   Wundt establishes psychological laboratory in Leipzig.

- 1905   First psychometric test produced by Binet and Simon.

- 1917   First military applications – US army alpha tests.

- 1921   National Institute of Industrial Psychology (NIIP) incorporated in the UK – active in test developments and applications.

- 1950s and 1960s   Tests widely used in commercial mass selection.

- Early 1970s   Reduction of commercial use of tests in the US following Equal Employment Opportunities Commission (EEOC) legislation and successful litigation.

- Late 1970s   Expansion of tests with clear occupational orientation.

- 1980s   Testing given a boost through the evolution of the competence movement.

- 1989   73 per cent of major UK companies using tests.

- 1991   British Psychological Society (BPS) institutes certification standards for test use and register of qualified occupational testers.

PSYCHOMETRICS EXPLORED

Mental measurement again

As we saw at the beginning of the chapter, actions arising from tests could be in a commercial setting supporting a selection or development decision. In educational settings tests are used to help determine actions in fields such as specific learning difficulties, and in counselling and career management they often help shape the direction of guidance being given. In all cases the psychometric test serves to provide a method that can be applied in a systematic way by different practitioners. Hence a key characteristic of a psychometric test is that it is standardised. Could there be measurement without standardisation?

Many of those considering the value of the standardisation offered by testing (eg Green 1981, Eysenck 1957) have almost immediately emphasised some of the issues and difficulties involved. The principal issues will be examined further in the course of this book.

Different forms of test

In essence information is given by a psychometric test through giving those taking the test the opportunity to respond to a series of items or events that relate directly or indirectly to a particular area of behaviour. The area can be a skill such as reasoning with numbers or an interpersonal behaviour such as a tendency to give support to other people.

Most common and familiar are those psychometric instruments that list a series of questions with alternative answers. The questions may involve propositions or statements as in the *16 Personality Factor Questionnaire*, known as the *16PF* (Cattell et al 1970) and the *OPQ – Occupational Personality Questionnaires* (Saville et al 1984), or can be in a form such as identifying which of a number of diagrams fits a set of other diagrams: eg the *Differential Aptitude Tests*, abstract spatial relationships test. (Note that although most of these tests do use questions as such, the more general term for what is presented is 'item'. This broader term encompasses statements to be agreed with or choices between pairs of self-descriptive statements.)

In other tests the response required is in the form of an

interpretation of pictures. In the well-known *Ishihara Colour Blindness Test* responses are in the form of recognition of hidden figures. Yet other tests may require responses using wooden blocks or other physical material to match patterns (eg Wechsler 1955). Psychometric tests involving tasks such as tracking a moving target have long been used in the selection of civil and military aircrews. An early NIIP test for assessing driving ability developed a form of driving simulator. When the candidate driver crashed the vehicle a sandbag was dropped on one end of a pivoted plank. The other end of the plank was thereby forced up to strike the driving seat from below!

Tests and non-tests

Thus tests vary in form and it is the systematic approach rather than the form itself that is key. Certain standards in the construction of a test are also necessary for it to be truly regarded as a proper psychometric instrument. Such standards are promulgated and supported by bodies such as the British Psychological Society (BPS) or American Psychological Association (APA) and essentially cover the research requirements necessary to set up a psychometric test. These include the development of an appropriate and systematic means of interpretation. Without such standardised methods tests are of little practical use.

This subject will be returned to in Chapter 6. However, for now it should be noted that the existence of such standards does not provide absolute guarantees. Regulation of test design has little of the force applied in other areas of activity that impinge upon people, such as food and drugs. A number of tests widely used commercially have from time to time been questioned as to their fitness for use but without any clear responsibility for, and hence little chance of, remedial action. There is, too, still considerable soul-searching among psychologists and others professionally involved in testing as to what procedures and forms of use are proper and representative of best practice. For instance Feltham, in a paper current at the time of writing (Feltham et al 1994) claims that bad selection decisions should be more commonly attributed to inappropriate use of tests than to the tests themselves being inherently bad.

Casually produced sets of questions without appropriate research backing cannot be regarded as psychometric tests as such. However, the fact that in form of presentation what is printed in a magazine looks like a personality questionnaire supported by 20 years of research may well mislead the unwary, particularly when such instruments yield scores, as they often do.

Publication by a reputable publisher – such as those listed in Appendix 2 – although clearly not a defining characteristic of psychometrics, is one fairly reliable guide. It should be noted though that many effective and respectable testing procedures are also produced within commercial organisations or university departments. Bodies such as the civil service have operated with their own test batteries for many years. In all cases the typical pattern has included processes of research to test out the individual items and then gathering these together in a whole test.

Graphology – a persistent case

Of the procedures that should not be regarded as constituting psychometric testing, but which are often wrongly associated with it, graphology, the interpretation of handwriting, is the most common. The means of interpretation used never seems to have been subjected to rigorous statistical treatment, certainly not in a way to accord with the design standards applied to the general body of psychometrics. Eysenck (1957) and Mackenzie Davey over 30 years later (1989), after reviewing research on handwriting analysis, cast doubt on the scientific nature of the approach. (The latter does report research showing it to be an effective guide to gender, but also reports the researcher concerned as being doubtful as to the value of this finding!)

Why it has continued to be used at all is a matter for speculation. There is probably an element of 'it would be nice if it did work'. That it continues to command the attention of professional psychologist researchers probably reflects a 'grain of truth' argument. All manifestations of behaviour are linked to some extent. Handwriting patterns could be expected to reflect muscular tension, among other things. Muscular tension might well reflect a general anxiety level. However the grain of truth fails to reveal itself in any adequate scientific demonstration!

HOW TESTS ARE USED TODAY – SELECTION TO COUNSELLING

In selection, tests are commonly used as part of a chain of activity, but their positioning in the chain may vary substantially. At one extreme is their use as an early stage screening process in procedures such as apprentice or graduate recruitment. The idea is to pass on those with a relatively high chance of success for further examination. At the other extreme is their use at much later stages. For example, executive recruitment firms will often suggest psychometric procedures be applied to shortlist candidates to extend information already available on them. Often this will be to acquire a view as to how the candidates might fit with other members of a management team.

Tests may also be applied within an organisation in ways comparable to those used in external recruitment. The results of tests used in these circumstances will be seen as part of the information to aid management in making a decision as to the suitability of an internal appointee. In other cases the application of a test would represent a contribution to development planning and providing the individuals with greater insights into themselves in concert with procedures such as workshops or development centres. In these cases the test results might be seen either as essentially for the private use of the person tested and his or her mentors or as part of a company database, for use, say, for manpower or training resource planning.

Vocational guidance and counselling of individuals in relation to performance improvement or to give advice on career management are other uses overlapping with development planning. Tests are also often used in counselling individuals who are actually or potentially redundant. They may be utilised to look at particular abilities and aptitudes or to help inform discussions on aspirations by concentrating on particular areas of interest.

VALIDITY AND RELIABILITY

Much of what has been said above in relation to what is and what is not a test can be illustrated further through the exploration of test validity and reliability.

Validity refers to whether a test measures what it is supposed

a) Predictive validity - identifying future performance

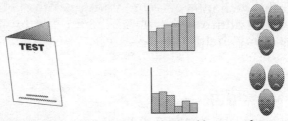

b) Concurrent validity - distinguishing higher and lower performers

c) Content validity - reflecting relevant material in the test

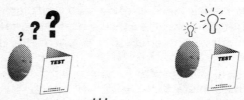

d) Face validity - appearing credible

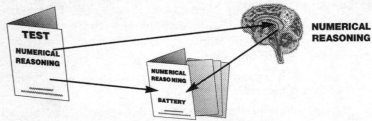

e) Construct validity - measuring what its supposed to measure

Figure 1.1 *The different types of validity*

to measure. *Reliability* refers to whether the measurement provided is consistent. Within these simple propositions, though, are a host of complications and traps for the unwary. Detailed requirements for test validity and associated matters are given in professional publications such as those issued by the American Psychological Association (1954). Some of these issues will be returned to in greater detail at specific points in the forthcoming chapters. For the moment the main types of validity will be addressed and explained briefly. Referring to Figure 1.1 may help the reader in understanding these important ideas.

Predictive validity

Very often tests are used to help determine suitability for a particular role. Thus inherent in their use is the idea of predicting behaviour and hence performance in the future. The predictive validity of a test is the extent to which it predicts future behaviour. To establish predictive validity requires scope for effective, controlled research over a period of time. This in turn implies fairly large numbers in the research samples, and some stability of roles and performance measures. Regrettably performance criteria are often wholly or partly undefined, subject to change over time and/or not supported by complete records. These issues were a fairly early concern (eg Stott 1950), but they do not go away, as the example below from the life insurance industry shows.

LIFE INSURANCE SUCCESS: THE MOVING TARGET

Life insurance has large numbers of people, lots of data and some history of using psychometric methods. The volume of business written by an agent would seem to be an obvious and objective criterion of success against which to check the predictive validity of a test.

However all is not plain sailing! Here are just a few of the complicating factors.

- Within the overall criterion of business volume the need for refinement of the criterion measure to reflect business cancelled at different times during the originally intended life of a policy.

- Differential ease of business by geographic area – city versus rural, affluent versus non-affluent, age of population.

- Changes of company organisation (at the time of writing mergers and takeovers are rife in this industry in the UK).

- Very high staff turnover.

- Varying competitor activity.

- Varying effectiveness of agents' managers.

- The practice of dividing up successful 'patches', giving part to new entrants.

- New products constantly coming on to the market.

- Changes in regulation – legal and industry-imposed affecting for example what can and cannot be said to clients, potentially impacting ease of sale.

In practice predictive validity studies tend only to be conducted by or with the cooperation of very large and relatively stable employers.

Another difficulty is the question of how predictive a test needs to be for it to be effective. This question will be returned to again in Chapters 6 and 8. For the moment it may be worth noting that even low levels of predictive validity can be useful in cases where the numbers to be selected are very small in relation to those being tested.

Concurrent validity

Given the difficulties of establishing predictive validity effectively, organisations more often undertake validation in the here and now. If a group of individuals established as high performers on a job are found to produce high scores on a test, with the low job performers producing correspondingly low test scores, then effective concurrent validity has been established. Thus concurrent validity is the extent to which a test score differentiates individuals in relation to a criterion or standard of performance external to the test. As with predictive validity the criterion itself has to be established. However, what is required minimally is agreement on who should fit into which of two fairly extreme groups. This is less demanding than considering more exactly what a person's score should be on some criterion measure as would ideally be the case with predictive validity. Nor, of course, is concurrent validity itself affected by changes in criteria of performance over time. (However, if such changes do occur they will imply a need to re-establish concurrent validity in the changed circumstances.)

Content validity

This form of validity indicates the way in which what is in the test directly represents aspects of a role or job. This again seems straightforward on the surface. However in the field of personality assessment the items cannot be over-transparent if, for example, the respondent is not to be able simply to project a socially desirable image. Hence the content validity of such items may be hard to establish.

Credibility and acceptance – face validity

Some of the controversies picked up from time to time in the press have focused on particular items from personality questionnaires that appear to be fanciful. Concern of this sort is concern for face validity, a particular aspect of content validity. If those responding to items find them bizarre they may fail to treat the whole process seriously. Whether this happens or not will depend in some measure not only on the item itself but also the manner and setting in which the whole testing process is conducted. Thus professional administration may well enhance face validity.

By the same token, of course, an unprofessional demeanour on the part of those delivering the test will detract from the face validity of the whole process, regardless of the particular items. Lack of face validity from whatever source, leading to a casual or overly cynical approach on the part of those undertaking the procedure, can clearly have a negative impact on other forms of validity. However, as with these other forms of validity, face validity cannot just be assumed and nor can its absence. I have seen old NIIP tests with items depicting women in Victorian hoop-skirted crinoline dresses being used with complete acceptance for the selection of railway clerks in a Third World country.

Construct validity

Construct validity is the extent to which a test measures a particular construct or characteristic. While predictive validity is concerned with the test in relation to an external criterion of performance, construct validity is, in effect, concerned with looking at the test itself. If a test is intended to measure, say, numerical reasoning, can evidence be found that suggests it is this that is being measured – is the construct of numerical reasoning as covered by the test valid? Such evidence might come from a number of sources.

One aspect of construct validity is the way in which the different test items in effect hang together. It should be possible to show that items do fit in with one or other particular construct. For example if a test has 20 items relating to the scale extroversion versus introversion, people endorsing an extroverted response on any one item should tend to endorse responses in the same direction on other items.

Establishing construct validity will often involve quite extensive studies, typically cross-referring to other tests. Staying with extroversion for the moment, part of establishing the construct validity of a new test of that characteristic would be to compare scores of individuals on that new test with their scores on one or more existing and well-established tests of extroversion.

INTRODUCTION TO PRACTICAL ISSUES IN CONTROL AND INTERPRETATION

Copyright to 'driving tests'

As indicated at the beginning of this chapter the control of test use has tended to increase over the years. In the UK test publishers have progressively been tightening their standards on distribution, for instance. There have been a series of successful prosecutions under breaches of copyright law and the BPS is continuing to develop standards for competency in test use.

As with many areas of professional usage and practice, however, the issue of decay of skills and keeping up to date with new developments has scarcely begun to be addressed. Thus we have the driving test phenomenon, whereby someone initially and effectively trained may not in fact practise interpretation procedures very frequently, and may not have their ongoing ability to perform at defined skill levels checked. In general, though, the professional position is tighter than it used to be and it seems not too optimistic to suppose that abuses will be progressively eradicated as the understanding of tests increases.

Own 'specialists' or consultants?

Organisations embarking on a programme of psychometric application will need to decide whether to spend time and money on having their own people trained in psychometrics or, alternatively, to use the services of a qualified consultant. The latter are listed in the appropriate registers such as that held by the BPS and will give firms access to a wide range of instruments. Fees will, of course, be commensurate with the professional services provided.

Even for those organisations having their own staff trained, there is a question of explanation of test results to others in the organisation who may well have a legitimate interest in them but will not have undergone training in test use. There are guidelines for this, such as the guide issued by the Institute of Personnel Management (IPM 1993). These are among the matters addressed in relation to regulation in Chapter 6 and in building a test application in Chapter 8.

Having thus surveyed the testing scene broadly and indicated the tips of some icebergs of issues and controversies around, we turn in the next chapter to a more detailed look at the types of psychometric instrument that are most commonly available and the types of information that they provide.

SUMMARY

- Psychometric tests are mental measurement devices.

- They consist of series of questions or items to which people respond.

- Proper tests are well researched and standardised, so that they can be interpreted on a consistent basis.

- Graphology, the study of handwriting, does not accord with psychometric standards.

- Testing has its roots in the late nineteenth and early twentieth century, and its practice today is widespread but scarcely universal.

- Occupational uses of tests include selection, development, vocational guidance, career management and identification of suitability for training.

- Tests need to be reliable – that is produce consistent responses.

- Tests need to be valid – that is actually measure what they are supposed to measure.

2

Types of psychometrics and their interpretation

THE RANGE OF PSYCHOMETRIC TESTS

There are many tests in print – somewhere in excess of 5000 in the English language alone. In practice a relatively small number of them are used with any frequency. This simplifies matters in one sense – some degree of mastery or at least awareness is possible for the non-professional user. On the other hand there can be problems associated with over-exposure of tests – an issue that will be returned to in Chapter 5 and in Chapter 8 when constructing a psychometric application is considered.

Within the large number of tests altogether there are a few main types that differ in the type of information they provide. These types are described and considered here, while in Chapter 7 consideration is given to other types of instrument associated to various degrees with psychometric tests. Such instruments differ in form and design but overlap with psychometric tests in areas of application.

Within the mainstream of testing useful distinctions are made between measures used for assessing personality and those for assessing ability or attainment. Within these groups there are further distinctions among different categories of test, some of which will be considered in the immediately ensuing sections. Other distinctions among tests relate to aspects of their interpretation and these are discussed in the second part of this chapter, when interpretation is considered in general.

PERSONALITY MEASUREMENT

Questionnaires

The measurement of personality has, as indicated in the last chapter, been a matter of active interest for many years. It has long been recognised that personality is of great importance in a person's success in work, no less than in the approach they take to other aspects of their life. Personality measurement is very clearly part of the whole field of testing, but the way in which personality measures are labelled and described varies. The American Psychological Association in its technical recommendations (1954) suggested that the term 'questionnaire' rather than test should be generally used in the title of personality measures. This applied particularly to measures requiring responses to a series of self-descriptive items such as 'I like to attend family gatherings ... TRUE, IN BETWEEN, FALSE'.

The argument runs that such instruments do not test behaviour directly, but rather how the respondent chooses to describe his behaviour. It has also been argued (eg by Cronbach 1964) that such questionnaires or self-report inventories, as they are sometimes known, indicate typical behaviour. There are no right or wrong answers as such and these measures are contrasted with ability tests, where there are right and wrong answers, and where the whole focus is upon how high a score can be achieved.

The wisdom of this argument can be questioned in the sense that there certainly are right and wrong personality mixes for certain jobs. However, for the moment it is worth noting that the usage of the term 'questionnaire' in titles is common, but not universal, and the term 'test' is widely used in describing such instruments. For example in Heather Birkett Cattell's excellent guide to *The 16PF*, *Personality in Depth* (1989), both usages appear on the same page. In this book the general practice then, will, be to use the term 'questionnaire' in relation to titles and specific references to self-report personality instruments, but to continue to use the terms 'tests', 'testing' and 'psychometrics' more generally in discussing them.

Traits, types and factors

Personality measures look at characteristic ways in which individuals behave both on their own and in relation to the world about them. Sometimes these characteristics are referred to as 'traits'. The term 'factors' is also used. This tends to be reserved for characteristics established by the statistical techniques known as 'factor analysis' (see Appendix 1).

Very often such tests are of interest in occupational settings because of the insights they give into characteristic behaviour of one person in relation to another or to a group of others. Scales such as 'wanted inclusion' in the *FIRO-B* (Schutz 1978), 'group-dependent versus independent' in the *16PF* and 'sociability' in the *Gordon Personal Profile* are examples. Insights can also be given into such occupationally relevant areas as 'conscientious-ness' (*16PF*) or 'need for achievement' (*Edwards Personal Preference Schedule – EPPS*).

Taken as a whole such tests can clearly give clues to managers as to how a particular individual may be best supported or motivated. For example, a person showing a need to be controlled (*FIRO-B*) will not respond well by being given an entirely free hand.

Many personality questionnaires have been designed on the basis of psychological theory of personality. For example the *Myers Briggs Type Indicator* (*MBTI*) is based upon the theory of psychological types expounded by Jung. According to this theory people's responses to the world, ie their personality, reflect among other things the way in which judgements are made, whether logical or emotional – and the way in which information is processed, by sensation or intuition. The *Edwards Preference Schedule* is based on the theory of needs developed by Murray (1938) and lists 15 different need areas, including the need for achievement, the need for autonomy or independence, and the need for affiliation or to be doing things with friends.

The various different theoretical starting points are based on very different views of personality. However, what is becoming increasingly claimed is that a small number of personality dimensions is sufficient to account for much of the variation in behaviour classified under the heading of personality. This number is usually five and the term 'big five' is often applied. Although the labels of the five dimensions vary, one set gaining some degree of agreement is extroversion, agreeableness, conscientiousness, neuroticism and intellect. This relatively simple list may provide a frame of reference for what can be a bewildering array of individual scales and dimensions (31 scales in the Saville and Holdsworth Ltd's (SHL) *Occupational Personality Questionnaire*, 15 in the *EPPS* and 16 of course in the *16PF*). However, the finer grain of the larger number of scales will often help important distinctions to be made when comparing and contrasting individuals. We return to this issue a little later on in considering the interpretation of tests.

Projective techniques

Not all personality assessment involves the use of self-report methods. Projective techniques are based on the idea that an individual's perception of the world about him is coloured by his own personality. That is a person projects his personality upon the various stimuli that impinge upon him, making sense of them in at least a partially subjective way. At the level of common discourse we have the optimist characterised as one who sees his glass as half full and the pessimist as one who sees it as half empty. The glass and the present amount of its contents are the same in each case but the personality – optimistic or pessimistic – is projected upon it.

The idea of projection is rooted in the work of Freud and the other nineteenth-century psychoanalysts. It has given rise to a number of psychometric procedures, in various formats. One such is the *Rorschach Test* (1942). This is made up of a number of ink blots, to which the respondent responds by saying what they look like. Responses are scored for a range of attributes, including emotionality and imagination. Despite much research the validity of this particular test has remained doubtful. Later variants that have stressed a more detailed analysis of the content of responses have appeared more promising (eg Holt 1958).

Other approaches use pictures with ambiguous situations. For instance some of these can be interpreted as threatening. Failure to recognise the threats is seen as evidence of a general tendency to cope with threatening situations by denial. Such tendencies can be seen as particularly counterproductive for occupations involving a high degree of risk, such as fast jet pilots or commodity brokers, where threats need to be recognised and accurately weighed up.

Some of the most extensive development with such ambiguous material has been that of Murray with the *Thematic Apperception Test* (1943). This consists of a series of cards on which the ambiguous pictures are presented. The person being tested is required to make up a story about each picture and the content of this is then subjected to a systematic analysis. This approach has since been developed into the various techniques for analysing motivation through looking at the content of responses, which are discussed in Chapter 7.

The interpretation of most projective techniques is highly skilled, with single instruments sometimes requiring months or years of study. They are, therefore, less likely to form part of the routine toolkit of management embarking on psychometrics than many of the other methods referred to in this book. They are, though, worth noting for possible use in specialised applications, for example, in the selection of people for physically risky occupations or those trading in enormous sums of money.

ABILITY, APTITUDE AND ATTAINMENT

Job specific and less specific

The terms *aptitude* and *ability* are not always precisely separated. Many tests in these categories are used to look at behaviour, often of an intellectual or cognitive nature with greater or lesser degrees of specificity. Thus there are tests of general intelligence, that can be regarded as mental horse power or the general ability to process information and more specialised tests of particular ability, eg verbal reasoning. The term *aptitude* is usually reserved for those tests directed at predicting whether skill in a particular area can be acquired. Examples are the *Computer Operator Aptitude Battery (COAB)* and clerical aptitude batteries such as that in *SHL's Personnel Test Battery*.

The term ability tests tends to be reserved for measures of less job-specific though often still job-related intellectual characteristics. Examples are the various critical reasoning tests, eg *Watson-Glaser Critical Thinking Appraisal*, number ability tests (eg *SHL's NM* series) and tests of abstract reasoning such as *Raven's Progressive Matrices*. Although the distinction between ability and aptitude is not always made fully in the description of tests, this whole group is broadly separated from the personality questionnaires by describing them as tests of maximum rather than typical performance.

A range of item formats found in ability tests is shown in Figures 2.1 to 2.3. Different types of problem or task are posed, tapping into different abilities and at different levels of difficulty. Simple items of the type shown in Figure 2.1 might be used in tests for shopfloor selection. Figure 2.2 shows items typical of those used in clerical recruitment. Items requiring extraction of data from complex numerical and verbal material, as illustrated in Figure 2.3, would form reasoning tests such as

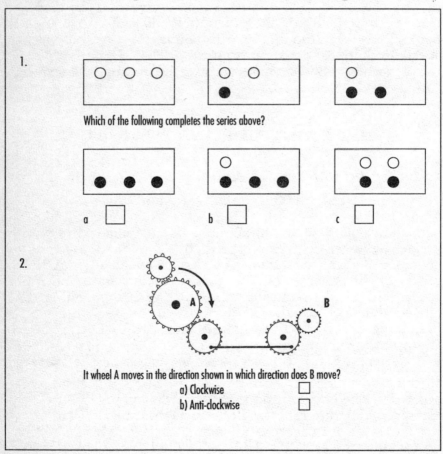

Figure 2.1 *Test items in abstract and spatial format*

1.   A B C D X F G H J

ABCDEFGHX   ☐

ABCDEPQRS   ☐

ABECXFGHJ   ☐

ABCDXFGHJ   ☑

ABHDXFGJH   ☐

Tick the series on the right which corresponds exactly to the one on the left.

2.   John prefers tea to coffee and likes coffee less than mineral water. If offered a choice between mineral water and tea, which would he be most likely to choose?

a. ☐   b. ☐   c. ☐
tea   mineral water   can't say

3.   Choose the number from the right to complete the series on the left

1 5 17 53   161   112   98

Figure 2.2 *Simple checking and reasoning items*

are used in graduate and managerial selection and development.

Although many tests do focus on particular characteristic abilities there is interest in the issue of how intelligence in general is constituted. Work by Carroll (1980), for instance, has endeavoured to look at how separate intellectual abilities can best be described by examining in detail the types of intellectual task imposed in different types of test. As indicated in Chapter 1 such issues have in fact been an ongoing concern of psychometrics since the early days and are still discussed today. (See for example Irvine et al 1990.)

In the centrally planned state of Rurigraria farmers are given subsidies by the Agrigulture Ministry to grow certain crops. If they achieve production quotas they also receive a production bonus. Subsidies and quota levels vary by size of farm and crop grown. The table shows the amount of money paid out in a four year period. The national unit of currency is the zipka.

Farm Size

Year	Under 200 hectares				200 to 1,000 hectares				over 1,000 hectares			
	1	2	3	4	1	2	3	4	1	2	3	4
Grapes: Subsidy	155	165	360	360	1,000	1,000	1,500	1,800	20	30	10	40
Bonus	10	25	30	40	10	200	150	200	10	80	90	100
Brassicas: Subsidy	50	60	60	60	45	0	35	0	80	80	80	80
Bonus	70	30	30	50	30	20	100	110	45	80	70	75
Corn: Subsidy	50	50	0	0	400	600	800	700	50	170	180	200
Bonus	200	200	20	0	800	1,000	1,200	1,500	300	400	450	600

Notes: 1. All figures in 000,000 zipkas
2. Grape vines planted in Rurigraria take four years to become productive
3. Brassicas and corn can be harvested in the year of planting

Answer the following:

	Definitely True	Probably True	Can't Say	Probably False	Definitely False
1. Some farmers grew grapes before the start of the four year plan.	☐	☐	☐	☐	☐
2. There are few large farms	☐	☐	☐	☐	☐
3. The largest amount paid out to the small farmers was in year 3	☐	☐	☐	☐	☐

Figure 2.3 *Complex reasoning items*

A range of formats

The ability tests referred to so far in this chapter largely use series of items, or questions sometimes, as illustrated in Figures 2.1 to 2.3, involving interpretation of diagrams or charts. As indicated in Chapter 1, there are other formats though. Reference was made there to tests involving complex apparatus, such as those for hand–eye coordination used in pilot selection.

Ability tests have also been delivered using cine-film (see, for example, Ridgway 1977) and, of course today, increasing numbers are computer-driven, with items displayed on a screen. Although paper and pencil methods are still the most common they do not, then, represent the totality of ability tests.

Attainment tests

Often referred to as achievement tests these are somewhat more commonly used in relation to educational assessment than in occupational settings. They represent standard ways of assessing the amount of skill currently reached or attained in a particular area. For example, the *Foundation Skills Assessment* (*FSA*) published by The Psychological Corporation (1988) is designed to measure attainment in numeracy and literacy skills in adults. This battery of four tests is organised at three levels of difficulty for each and with a short initial screening test. The latter means that the appropriate level of difficulty can be chosen for detailed investigation and so the actual level of attainment assessed with some precision.

In the past many occupational applications of attainment tests have been in relation to blue-collar jobs, for instance to see if remedial educational training was required during initial periods of apprenticeship. However, recently comparable needs have arisen in some other fields. These are not yet evidently addressed by what could be called psychometric methods as such but are, nevertheless, worth noting. The Life Assurance and Unit Trust Regulatory Organisation (LAUTRO) requires certain knowledge in those representing financial organisations and gives guidance on how this might be assessed. Some life insurance companies have developed procedures for identifying such knowledge, ie how much of it has been achieved to date, in candidates, taking them through procedures that may be regarded as capable of further formal psychometric development.

Public examinations such as GCSE are also tests of attainment, measuring a combination of knowledge and abilities in manipulating and interpreting knowledge. They are standardised, but not developed according to psychometric criteria as such.

Adaptive testing

The selection of progressive levels of difficulty, as described above in connection with the *FSA*, is fundamental to adaptive testing. By using computers to score responses instantly, performance levels on tests can be monitored and difficulty levels adjusted. In this way the maximum level of performance can be more finely ascertained than with a fixed set of items. However, despite having been around for over a decade and also despite the increased use of computers in test administration, such tests have not yet found widespread use.

Trainability tests

Trainability tests are designed for use in those situations in which there is a definite and distinct course of training to be undertaken before a job can be executed. They, therefore, constitute one type of aptitude test and tend to have very specific applications. Many of them have been developed in relation to roles in which motor, that is physical, coordination is one requirement. A survey conducted in 1988 in the UK (Bevan and Fryatt 1988) suggested that although the bulk of the use of trainability tests lay in manual occupations, there were some applications in managerial fields.

Such tests began to be developed in the 1970s in relation to roles as wide apart as dentists, operators of heavy equipment in forestry or shipbuilding apprentices. (See, for example, Downs 1973, and Smith and Downs 1975.)

They have, perhaps, become separated from other forms of aptitude test because of their very close identification with very specific roles, even down to an individual factory, say, employing unique machine configurations. However, it is arguable that an instrument such as a computer programming battery with subtests such as comprehension of flow charts could be viewed in the same way. Thus, effective comprehension would be regarded as an indication of scope to master training involving flow diagrams.

Some trainability tests may also be seen as related to trade tests – measures of attainment – directly simulating samples of work. Examples include tests of stenography such as that produced by Seashore and Bennett as far back as 1948, and more currently the *Typing Test For Business* (Doppelt et al 1984), which sets copy-typing tasks.

INTEREST INVENTORIES

A number of psychometric test procedures have been developed specifically for aiding career guidance and career management planning although, in fact, a wide range of tests including personality and ability measures may be relevant. Of the specific tests some look at preferences for particular types of activity and then develop scales that relate these back to occupational groupings. Sometimes their results will suggest occupational areas not previously considered by the person taking the test. In other cases they may help rule out a type of occupation. I can recall a case of a redundant employee in a high tech company, referred for counselling. The man expressed an interest in farming as a new career. Farming did not, however, feature very highly on the list of likely occupations as revealed by his responses to an occupational interest inventory. Closer examination showed that he had a marked dislike of getting up early in the morning.

With tests cast in a purely abstract format, such as those illustrated in Figure 2.1, the items have no particular topicality. Other tests can, though, have items that relate to everyday life. For example, numerical reasoning tests will often present items in the form of financial data. Such items are, of course, likely to become dated from time to time.

In the case of occupational interest inventories the issue of obsolescence of items is, though, compounded by the changing nature of occupations. This can happen both in a growth sense, as certain industries decline and others are born, but also in relation to shorter term cyclical patterns which will clearly affect the availability of employment in different areas. Thus particular care is required in using such tests for guidance. Test publishers do take trouble to update the inventories themselves and the way in which they are interpreted occupationally. For example, the *Strong Inventory*, originally published over 50 years ago (see Strong 1943), has been much updated over the years with the latest edition supported by descriptions of over 100 current occupations.

INTERPRETING TEST RESULTS

The idea of norms

Very often a test result is interpreted for an individual in terms of how that individual stands relative to the scores achieved by a group on whom that test was standardised – the so-called norm group. The group may be identified as a large part of the population, eg UK adult males, or could be a subgroup of particular interest, eg sales managers in high technology companies or direct entry graduates. In either case the comparison yields a numerical score. The most common way in which this is expressed is as a *percentile*. For example to say that someone is at the eightieth percentile means that he or she produced a score in excess of that produced by 80 per cent of the comparison group and that 20 per cent of the comparison group scored higher. Thus the higher the percentile the higher the standing on the test concerned.

Such comparisons are very commonly made in the case of ability tests and norms are available for many personality questionnaires too. These latter are typically made up of a number of dimensions or scales and so the norm tables give relevant figures for each scale. Again these norms may relate to general population groups or be developed for particular categories, such as managers. For example Bartram (1992) has produced norms for the *16PF* for shortlisted managerial candidates. They provide a common way of thinking about relative scores among individuals on a single test and a language for relating scores of one individual from one test to another. On their own, though, they do not say very much. Even a percentile comparison related to a specific occupational group, eg the sales managers, again does not give a very direct indication of the likely effectiveness of the managerial candidate concerned. What it does tell us is, first, simply that person's standing *vis-à-vis* others in a similar occupational group, eg in the top 10 per cent or bottom 10 per cent. Second, provided the test has been shown to have some predictive or concurrent validity, it indicates that the higher the score the higher the relative chance of effective performance against the criterion of success used in the validation.

The normal curve

A number of other fundamental statistical ideas need to be introduced to help understand comparisons among test scores further. One of these is the *normal* curve. This curve (see Figure 2.4) describes the relationship between a set of observations or measures and their frequency of occurrence. Observations could be height, weight or, as in the case of interest here, scores on psychometric tests. The very wide range of application of the curve in relation to the study of people was originally explored by the nineteenth-century scientist Francis Galton. Interpreted simply and obviously it indicates that on many things one might care to measure a few people will produce extremely

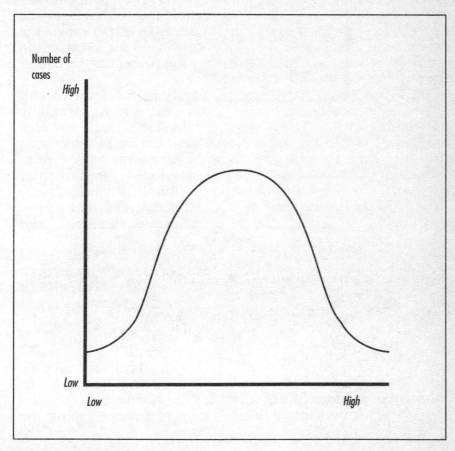

Figure 2.4 *The normal curve*

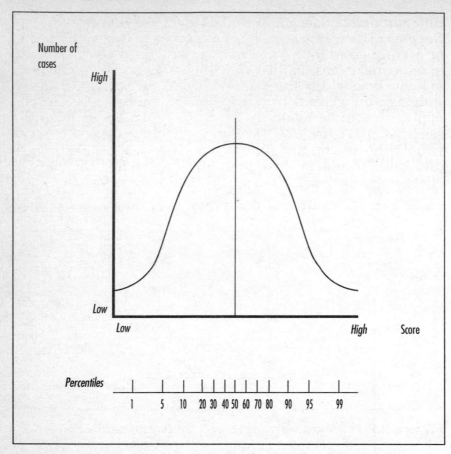

Figure 2.5 *The normal curve and percentile distribution*

high scores, a few extremely low and there will be a large bulk in the middle. (See Appendix 1.)

In Figure 2.5 percentiles have been plotted in relation to the normal curve. The fiftieth percentile point lies at the middle of the normal distribution so that half the area under the curve lies to the left and half to the right of that point.

The importance of variability

Test results are also very often interpreted in terms of units which are related to the variability found within the scores of the norm group. Let us say that on a 40-item reasoning test two different individuals got 28 and 32 right respectively – we say these were their raw scores. Let us also suppose that the mean or average score for a large number of individuals was 30. In order to make sense of this four-point difference we would need to know how widely the scores varied in our normative group. Although the general bell shape of the normal curve should apply, it could be relatively flat as in Figure 2.6 or relatively steep as in Figure 2.7. In Figure 2.6 there is much more variability among the scores in general, so a four-point difference would be less indicative of a real difference in effective performance than in the case represented in Figure

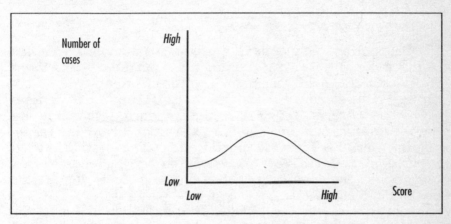

Figure 2.6 *Flattened normal curve – scores spread*

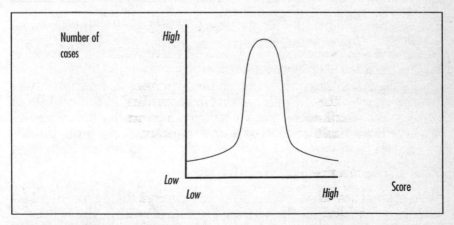

Figure 2.7 *Steep normal curve – scores clustered*

2.7. There, with tight clustering of scores, a four-point difference is much more meaningful. A far larger number of individuals would lie between 28 and 32 in this second case, so that the score difference would represent a greater difference in percentile terms.

Thus, just knowing that the scores were respectively two points above and two points below the mean does not tell us what we learn by taking variability into account. A test score recalibrated in terms of variability is called a derived score and such scores ease the making of comparisons among different results.

A range of derived scores

The basic measure of variability used is the standard deviation (for a more detailed explanation see Appendix 1). *Standard scores* indicate how far a person's score is from the mean score expressed in standard deviation units. These are sometimes known as z scores. Thus +1z is one standard deviation above the mean and -1z is one standard deviation below the mean, and the mean itself is represented by zero. These can be related to percentiles. Thus a score of one standard deviation unit, one z unit, above the mean equates approximately to the eighty-fourth percentile.

Unfortunately for the practically minded, rather than the merely curious, test user, a number of other derived scores, all based on means and standard deviations have arisen over the years. The most common of these are stanines and stens, but T scores and other derived scores are also used. All of these can be related back to the normal curve as shown in Figure 2.8.

- Z scores express scores in standard deviation units.

- Standard scores with a mean of 100 and 15 points are used sometimes, particularly in intelligence tests.

- Stanine is a contraction of standard nine. It has nine points. It uses a mean of 5 and assigns one point to each half standard deviation unit.

- Stens, now more commonly used than stanines, have a mean of 5.5 and similarly assign one point to each half standard deviation unit. The term means standard ten and the scale has ten points.

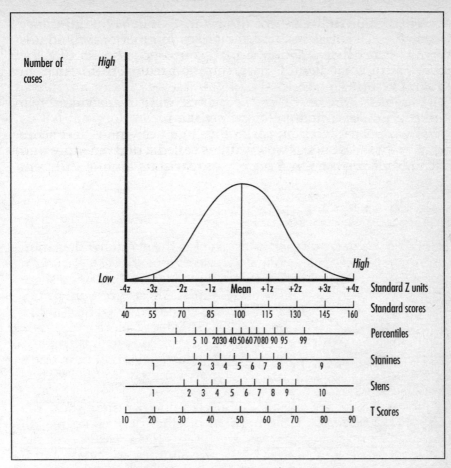

Figure 2.8 *The normal curve and derivative scales*

■ T scores have a mean of 50 and assign 10 points to each full standard deviation unit.

For further discussion of scoring see Appendix 1.

Skewed distributions

As well as being relatively flat (Figure 2.6) or relatively steep (Figure 2.7), in practice the normal curve may be distorted or skewed to the left or right. Figure 2.9 shows a case of what is known as negative skew. There are lots of high scores and few low ones. The test is relatively easy and might fail to give useful differentiation among those taking it. This could occur with a test, say, of spatial reasoning ability, developed and normed with a general population sample but applied to a group of astronaut candidates. If the group had been pre-screened on ability to pilot an aircraft the remaining candidates might well all perform near the top end of the test, limiting its value as an effectively discriminating aid to selection.

The opposite situation, positive skew, is shown in Figure 2.10. Here the test scores are crowded towards the bottom end – most of those taking the test found it too difficult.

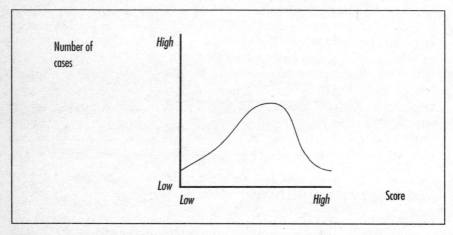

Figure 2.9 *Negative skew*

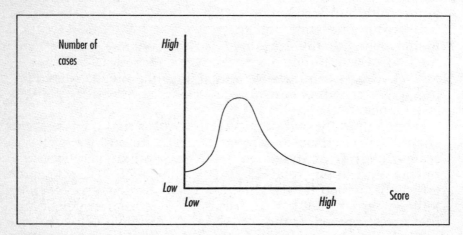

Figure 2.10 *Positive skew*

Interpreting multiple scores

For those aptitude and ability tests arranged in batteries, eg the *Computer Programmer Aptitude Battery* (*CPAB*), interpretation will involve reference to norms for each of the constituent tests. Interpreting the resultant patterns of scores may include considering how far a particular weakness can be compensated for by a particular strength. This is an issue to which we return in Chapter 4.

Multiple scores can also be obtained from individual ability tests divided into subtests. One example is the *Watson–Glaser Critical Thinking Appraisal* (1991), which is made up of five separate subtests posing different types of complex verbal reasoning tasks. Here the usual guidance is to concentrate on overall rather than subtest scores. There are two reasons for this. First there may be insufficient information in the relatively small number of items in the subtest to give a reliable, that is repeatable, score indication. Second, with those tests that are timed – as many are – some people will just not get as far as the later subtests. Guidance on whether or not subtest scores should be used is typically given in test manuals.

Scoring personality questionnaires

As indicated already, multiple scores also arise in relation to the various scales of personality questionnaires. Very often items on such questionnaires are arranged so that choices are made among alternative statements. Of a pair of such alternatives one will favour one scale and the other a second. Such arrangements mean that the scales are, of course, not independent. This method of combining items leads to what is called *ipsative scaling*. This is contrasted with the so-called *normative scaling*, in which strength of agreement to each item is rated separately (see Figure 2.11).

It is commonly said of ipsative measures that interpretation should be based on looking at patterns among the different scales, solely on an individual basis, rather than by reference to norms and their related statistics as such. Despite such criticisms, which have sometimes been strongly expressed (eg Johnson et al 1988), it is common for ipsative personality measures, as well as those based on normative items to have published scale norms associated with them. The debate will no

---

Tick which box describes you best

	Yes	In between	No
1. I like to spend time outdoors	☐	☐	☐
2. I prefer my own company	☐	☐	☐
3. I like a good laugh	☐	☐	☐

a. Normative scaling

1.1 I am sometimes aggressive to others ☐
1.2 I can work hard when necessary ☐

2.1 I dislike detail ☐
2.2 I stick to my point in debate ☐

3.1 I want to spend time with clever people ☐
3.2 I dislike people who make cynical remarks ☐

Tick which one of each pair describes you best

b. Ipsative scaling

Figure 2.11 *Normative and ipsative items*

doubt continue, with some writers (eg Saville and Wilson 1991) arguing strongly for the validity of both scaling approaches.

Trade-offs and patterns in personality measurement

Certainly personality measures do require very careful inter-pretation, with an examination of patterns among the scales. Consider the following case. Suppose that two of the scales of a personality questionnaire related to a preference for handling detail and an orientation to service respectively. Let us say that we were using the questionnaire to assist in recruitment for order processing clerks responding to incoming customer telephone calls. A person low on the former scale and high on the latter might be disappointing. The intention to provide good service would not be followed through in practice. A person high on detail handling but low on service orientation might fail to convince customers that he was actually going to respond to their needs, even though execution of specific clerical tasks might be perfect.

Again consider the executive candidate being looked at in relation to a business turn-round situation. Someone high on tough mindedness, assertive and forthright as revealed by the *16PF* would be likely to start to make things happen. Whether they carried others with them or not, and so effectively sustained their initial impetus, might depend on their also being high in terms of warmth, tendency to trust and a controlled, self-disciplined approach. A candidate with the latter but not the former group of strengths might create good feeling but few results.

Gaining an effective mastery of the interpretation of such patterns – typically of course with far more scales than in the examples just given – will take considerable training and practice. In order to reduce the complexity to manageable proportions there have been some interesting short-cut developments. Krug (1981) working with the *16PF* pointed out that if each of the 16 scales is presented as a sten value, then there are 10 to the power 16 or 10,000 billion possible combinations. In order to reduce the resultant complexity to less astronomical proportions he chose to work with 4 higher order accumulations of the 16 scales. He then reduced the sten scale to low, middle and high bands (stens 1–3, 4–7 and 8–10 respectively) giving him 3 to the power 4 = 81 combinations. Word descriptions of each of these were then produced, indicating the interplay among the four higher order scales in each case.

Expert systems

A similar idea lies behind the notion of *expert system* reporting of personality questionnaire results. Skilled interpreters of the personality measure concerned produce a library of descriptors covering different levels on each of the measure's scales. They also cover the more common combinations of these under groups of scales and define a logic for selecting the appropriate mixes of descriptions. Descriptions and logic are captured in software, so that any combination of scores can yield a computer-generated narrative. An example of such a narrative report is given in Appendix 3.

Test scores and performance

The various types of validity discussed in the previous chapter and the ways of comparing test scores through norms are all relevant to the question of using tests to predict future performance. Note that validity cannot be regarded as established once and for all or universally for any particular test. Predictive validity would be a most effective guide in those cases in which another group was being recruited to do the same job under very similar circumstances as those upon whom the predictive study had been conducted. However strong predictive validity in one case would not by any means assure that in another case it could still be assumed.

This could be so even within the same organisation and in relation to jobs with the same titles, studied at different periods of time. Consider the case of wordprocessing.

From the mid to the late 1980s many organisations increased their use of information technology by leaps and bounds. One manifestation of this was in wordprocessing. Such systems typically include a 'spell-check'. A test of secretarial aptitude including spelling items might well have shown predictive validity – have predicted secretarial performance – prior to this innovation, but not thereafter.

During the transition to the new technology some people might well have been apprehensive about it (a condition known as technophobia). A measure of attitudes to change in general or to technology in particular might well have been more predictive of success at that time than the secretarial aptitude test. Later, as this technology becomes more commonplace, with a growing generation of the early computer-literate, such a measure again would fail to predict success.

In fact, concurrent validity studies in periods of transition showing statistical separation between higher and lower performers might not only be the best that could be managed but actually the most appropriate.

Availability of norms

Ideally a validity study should always have been undertaken in the occupational area of interest. However, if norms have been established for an occupational group of relevance and, in particular, if these are clearly differentiated from the general population norm then, even without a specific validity study as such, there are grounds for believing the test to be valid for the occupation concerned. The existence of such relatively local norms do not, though, give direct grounds for selecting any particular score as a cut-off level (that is a test score used as a decision point with those below it being rejected and those above it being passed on for further consideration).

In practice the gathering of norms can be tricky. One does not routinely have ready access to the relevant groups and for many occupations in any one firm or organisation numbers may be small. Even when people are available in numbers large enough to allow the necessary statistics to be computed, this is no guarantee of the representativeness of the sample used. In fact so-called general population norms have rather rarely been developed on the basis of a strict reflection of a population. (One exception has been the *16PF*. In its original UK norming (Saville 1972) and its current updated version (*16PF 5*) care has been taken to sample according to strict population parameters. In both cases the Office of Population Censuses and Surveys has been used to support this work.)

In the next chapters we delve deeper into the practicalities of psychometric test use, as we consider their application first in selection, then in development.

SUMMARY

- Self-report personality measures are commonly described as personality questionnaires.

- Personality questionnaires are typically constructed on the basis of different theories of personality.

- The big five personality dimensions are extroversion, agreeableness, conscientiousness, neuroticism and intellect.

- Projective personality measures use a variety of relatively unstructured stimuli to which people respond, projecting their personality on to them.

- Ability and aptitude tests are sometimes described as measures of maximum performance attainable, in contrast with the typical performance revealed by personality measures. The former look at a range of intellectual functions and are designed with varying degrees of occupational specificity.

- Ability tests may be grouped in batteries to cover a number of aspects of an occupation.

- Attainment or achievement tests look at levels of performance already reached.

- Adaptive tests vary the level of difficulty depending on responses given.

- Trainability tests look at a person's likely success in mastering a training course, as a prerequisite for performing a job.

- Interest inventories examine preferences among different roles, tasks or activities.

- Test results are typically interpreted by the use of norms, positioning the individual's performance in relation to that of others in a reference group.

- Percentiles indicate where an individual sits *vis-à-vis* members of the norm group.

- Various types of standard score look at performance calibrated in terms of the variability of scores found in the norm group.

- With multiple tests or multiple test dimensions interpretation requires careful consideration of patterns of scores. Relevant comparison groups for norm development may not always be available.

3

Tests and selection: the developing context

MASS TESTING TO TRIAL BY SHERRY

The use of psychometric tests in external selection represents the largest category of application in work-related situations. Practices vary greatly but a number of broad patterns of usage emerge. Some of these can be seen to have their roots in the earliest days of testing. In particular mass application of tests to large groups of candidates is still quite commonplace with echoes of the earliest US military experience, referred to in Chapter 1. In all cases there is at least implicit the idea that the test is providing information of value to the selection process. However, the role and status of that information, and its links with other sources, is rarely clearly stated and perhaps even more rarely understood.

One of the reasons why there is often confusion in the role of tests stems from a lack of clarity in the overall information gathering process being undertaken in selection and hence how they contribute to that process. It is, for example, by no means uncommon for one or more arbitrary procedures to be added into the total flow of information gathered without any very distinct view of how these themselves can contribute. Unstructured semi-social events, dubbed in some quarters 'trial by sherry' are often seen as important and worthwhile parts of a selection process. Calling a candidate back for an extra meeting – perhaps the finance director should see him after all – is also by no means uncommon. In such hazy arrangements it is not surprising that the contribution of any particular element, not least psychometric tests, will be unclear!

It will be an aim of this chapter to consider what information is commonly gathered in selection situations and how it is used, while in Chapter 4 we look in more detail at how information from tests as such can function in selection.

We shall look first at the elements alongside which tests are often deployed, considering a number of areas of personal specification and reviewing their place in the selection process.

SOME FAVOURITE MEASURES – CLUB MEMBERSHIP TO AGE

The purpose of any procedure used in selection is to find out something about the candidate or candidates that will be of relevance to their functioning in the job or role concerned. Note that this statement, for the moment, carefully avoids reference to functioning successfully or to objectively measured performance on the job. Such considerations are not always implicit in the minds of those making the selection! In fact it is evident that in many selection situations a primary consideration is getting someone who is 'one of us' or 'who I can get on with' without any specific identification of how such criteria are likely to be reflected in performance as such.

It is perhaps because such notions are representative of muddled and non-specific, rather than wrong thinking that they are rather difficult to understand and shift. Thus an implicit model of 'one of us' could have a fundamentally sound basis and be capable of representation in terms of behaviour. Consider, for example, a successful team of financial consultants dealing routinely face-to-face with customers to advise them on their affairs. An absence of particular superficial characteristics of speech – both accent and vocabulary – manner and style of dress could immediately brand the candidate as not 'one of us'. This lack could also impact upon the clientele in such a way that, in fact, the candidate would be unsuccessful in the role.

Rarely, if ever, is this formally researched and the extent to which the possession of other qualities, such as work rate, a positive attitude and ability with figures could compensate, may never be entertained or explored. This may be the case, even though in such circumstances it would be recognised that those lacking these other qualities – eminently capable of investigation by psychometrics – would fail.

Fiction and prejudice

Also, being one of us is not only part of the implicit model of success, but also may reflect feelings of discomfort not necessarily voiced directly, that would arise by admitting to employment and hence to what is in effect a social group, those with differing styles and mores. Maintaining the comfort factor by control of group membership is a powerful, if often unspoken, motivation. Fiction, from Shaw's *Pygmalion*, to Mark Twain's *A Connecticut Yankee at King Arthur's Court* has often projected the idea of the outsider making good through the use of capacities of real relevance to successful performance in the role. In such fiction these capacities are various, including ingenuity, tenacity and honesty. However the players in such dramas tend to battle against tremendous odds and the comic structure of such stories is one of the ways in which they can, comfortingly, be set apart from real life.

The power of implicit models is vividly illustrated in a lecture given by C S Myers, a grand old man of British psychology, 75 years ago (Myers 1920). In a comment made without explanation, let alone apology or mitigation reference is made by the doyen to the higher and lower races. The thinking supporting this view of the world – the implicit model – is clearly deeply embedded.

The experience trap

Over millenia the philosophically minded have commented wisely about the misleading nature of experience. Thus Hippocrates, 'Life is short ... experience treacherous' or Plato in relation to evil and the judge, 'Knowledge should be his guide, not personal experience'. More recently there is Wilde, 'Experience is the name most people give to their mistakes' and perhaps most appositely Shaw, 'Men are wise in proportion not to their experience, but to their capacity for experience'.

Yet in selection situations a number of years' experience of a particular role or activity is often equated with successful performance and comes to be regarded as an absolutely essential criterion.

Inputs and outputs

In practice what is happening here is that experience, either in terms of a number of years or in relation to, say, association with a particular procedure or process is treated as an output behaviour equivalent to, say, communications skills or ability to manage. In fact it is, rather, a piece of input information.

The fact that the information will, in many cases, have a poor power of prediction is not considered, perhaps partly because it is not understood to be functioning as a predictor of performance but is treated as if it were the performance itself. As a predictor it stands at best as a rough shorthand for past performance. Past performance may or may not be an effective predictor for future performance, depending among other things on the similarity between the target job and those in which the performance was demonstrated. (See Figure 3.1 for an illustration of these points.) If the reader will tolerate yet another quotation, consider Coleridge: 'Experience is like the stern lights of a ship, which illumine only the tracks they have passed'.

Like the mariners of old in their explorations, most people seeking new jobs are looking for career development. Ongoing job satisfaction is very often bound up with personal growth and self-actualisation. This usually means a move on to something bigger, better and different. If candidates were totally experienced in the job they were seeking to fill one would rightly be inclined to question their motivation. A new job is inevitably a new experience to a greater or lesser degree. The selector has to predict future performance.

(The whole picture is complicated further by the fact that some organisations see specific experiences as counter-indicators, which if not absolute will still weigh against a candidate. An example is that of salespeople in the insurance industry. Some employers will argue that in an industry with such a high staff turnover, the unsuccessful move on and the successful stay. Thus anybody now seeking to work in such a role, who has done so previously, is bound to be one of the unsuccessful ones!)

Experience versus psychometrics

Where experience is more clearly seen as input, rather than output, it is still often regarded as a separate entity from

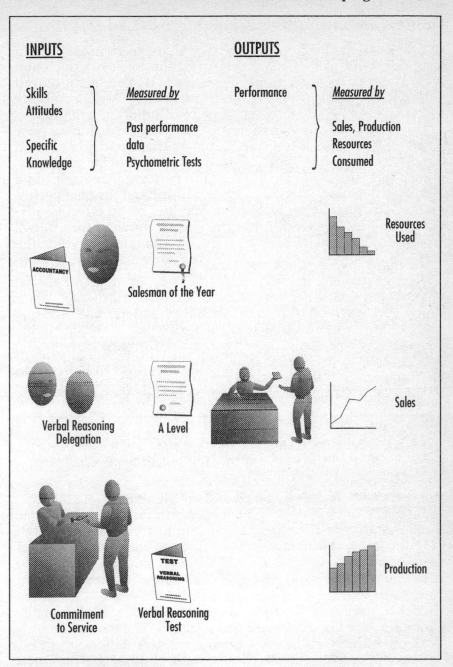

Figure 3.1 *Determining performance*

anything that might be measured by psychometrics. In fact, though, there is considerable scope for psychometric procedures or psychometric considerations to be brought into play here. For example if the role is considered to require the ability to apply experience in novel ways then tests relating to creativity (eg the *Cree Questionnaire* distributed by Science Research Associates) or style of information handling (eg the *Myers-Briggs Type Indicator*, referred to in Chapter 2) may be useful.

Experience is also often taken, of course, for a sign of explicit knowledge. Some organisations have gone down the track of actually testing such knowledge directly in what are, as referred to in Chapter 2, in intention if not in a strict scientific practice, tests of attainment. By a systematic application of such procedures the relevant knowledge is more fully explored than, say, in an interview.

In many selection situations, of course, activities are taken stepwise. Evidence of experience from a CV or application form means that that experience may be explored further in a later stage, very often an interview. Such exploration may, again, be related to the knowledge base of experience – which as just argued may be better explored by a more formalised method. It is also used to investigate other characteristics, in effect using the experience as the vehicle through which the candidate may demonstrate particular capacities, as in the following.

I see that you had a group of six people reporting to you when you were in the x,y,z company. Tell me something about how you helped them to succeed.

Working on the a,b,c, project in Ruritania sounds interesting. What were the most difficult situations that you encountered there?

The first of these passages indicates an interest in and concern for others and for staff development – capable of exploration through psychometric procedures such as *FIRO-B* or the *Edwards Personal Preference Scale* (*EPPS*). The second may be seeking evidence on handling complex information or attitude to work. Complex information handling could be measured through instruments such as *SHL's Critical Reasoning Tests*, while a tendency to be deeply involved in work and to drive through against difficulties could be assessed through the *Jenkins Activity Survey* (1979).

This is not, for the moment, to argue that these particular psychometrics would necessarily do a better job than the interview questions, but rather that information derived from experience is by no means the only way in which such evidence could be gathered!

The role of the interview

This book is about psychometrics and their use but, as should be manifest by now, seeks to set psychometrics in a practical context and help organisations think about their best use. The comments made so far have suggested more than once that psychometric procedures are likely to give more effective and appropriate information than other methods commonly used, such as the interview. We have already considered the idea of a comfort factor; an interview may supply this and as indicated above comfort is not necessarily wholly irrelevant in a consideration of someone joining an organisation.

Let us dwell for a moment on how the interview may contribute to the whole picture. (This is, of course, different from the more common way of proceeding by considering what psychometrics may add to the interview, the use of which is itself taken for granted.)

If an interview is conducted by the person for whom the candidate will be working directly it is likely to give indications of personal liking or rapport, or its absence. These indications may not be formally acknowledged and reflected in any competency description, which will tend to relate to a class of job rather than a specific one in many circumstances. Certainly once recruited people often fail in their work because they fail to get on with their bosses and it may quite often be more realistic for an interviewing manager to recognise that he actually does or does not like the candidate before him than to be told he should or should not like him on the basis of a personality instrument.

However, liking is not a guarantee of success. Very often a subordinate will need to have a complementary pattern rather than be cast in the same mould as his superior and he will, too, have to fit in with a number of other team members. Successive interviews with different interviewers may be popular largely because they often give different team members an opportunity to decide whether or not they would feel comfortable with the candidate joining the team.

Short term factors

The interview as an information gathering exercise is likely to be most effective in determining some of the aspects of the candidate that may be relatively short term or transitory. Present circumstances, motivations and financial expectations are much more amenable to this type of interaction than are elements of personality or higher level mental functioning. Conversely, information on personality or reasoning, although pointing to behaviour such as competitiveness and practical problem solving, will not address the specific personal circumstances, which the interview can.

Candidates will, too, tend to have a variety of questions to ask of an employer and will often wish to form a view as to their level of liking of them as individuals and as representatives of the hiring organisation.

For the moment note that it is a commonplace that all drivers think they are excellent drivers and all interviewers excellent interviewers. Although I have experienced the wry smiles and knowing nods that greet this proposition when included in discussions with management groups, I can only recall one manager ever who volunteered that he was, in fact, a poor interviewer! We are all apparently experts on people, with many of us having gained our expertise in the great university of life. We return to interviewing again later, particularly in Chapter 7.

Age

The specification of age in selection situations is, sadly, not yet illegal in the UK. It is in the US and Canada, while in France recruitment advertisements may not by law state an upper age restriction. Like other discriminators, such as race and sex, the use of which are now outlawed, age is quite apparently and conveniently determined. Just like experience, age seems to carry with it implications of behaviour. However, also like experience it is at best an input to behaviour but is often confused with behavioural outputs.

Some organisations claim to have established that only individuals in certain age bands – sometimes defined as narrowly as a period of four years – have been found to succeed in the role concerned. Figures are rarely quoted in support of such assertions. One frequent argument is that only individuals over a certain age will have the necessary experience but, of course, this falls back upon the arguments relating to experience once more. In fact if age is only working through experience it will be a weaker predictor than is that weak predictor.

JOB DEFINITIONS TO COMPETENCIES*

The role of job definitions

Defining the job in terms of duties and responsibilities or in terms of outputs, performance and accountabilities has often been helpful in thinking about the appropriate use of tests in selection. Such statements will often define what is required to be done in the job and/or may indicate qualities and capacities necessary to perform successfully. Sometimes the statements of what is required are quite detailed. Where standards of performance, rather than vaguely expressed areas of operation, are indicated they may give quite a ready read across to the way in which measurement may be carried out. This is illustrated in the extract from a job definition overleaf.

---

* Note that spelling varies here. While competency with the plural competencies appears most common, some organisations favour, and even insist upon, competence and competences.

Job Title: Senior Engineering Manager

....

Dimensions: Factory operations on three sites.

Budgeted spend: £12m.

Total strength: 180 personnel.

Direct reports: 5 engineering managers, quality manager, head of materials purchasing, secretary.

Special considerations: After the recent run-down and the concentration of manufacturing on the present three sites from five previously, there is a need to rebuild morale among the engineering workforce. The company has identified total quality management (TQM) as a spearhead initiative in continuing to drive down on costs and to increase competitiveness through enhanced customer service at all levels.

The person appointed must:

(a) be able to translate the company's TQM policy into effective action through identifying appropriate techniques and critical areas for their initial application;

(b) be able to build a team quickly;

(c) be quick to identify strategic implications of variances from the cost containment plans;

(d) have the energy and sense of responsibility to put in extra effort to 'pump-prime' the necessary new initiatives.

Broad band personality questionnaires such as the *16PF* or *SHL's OPQ* would yield information on many of these areas – team building, innovation, a rational approach to data could all be covered. The special considerations section indicates the importance of customer service, and those instruments and scales indicating conscientiousness would be relevant here. The enthusiastic scale of the *16PF* would be relevant in considering the rebuilding of morale and forward planning in the *OPQ* would be of relevance in translating TQM policy into action.

The reasoning skills indicated might be assessed by an instrument such as the *Watson-Glaser Critical Thinking Appraisal*.

Checklists

Sometimes in developing a job definition use is made of a checklist of characteristics such as the one below.

- Individual characteristics:
  —achievement drive;
  —entrepreneurial inclination;
  —personal commitment;
  —energy;
  —self-confidence;
  —flexibility.

- Interpersonal characteristics:
  —listening;
  —negotiation skills;
  —oral communications;
  —written communications;
  —charisma;
  —service orientation.

- Intellectual characteristics:
  —rapid learning;
  —strategic conceptualisation;
  —pattern recognition;
  —verbal reasoning;
  —numerical reasoning;
  —innovation.

- Managerial characteristics:
  —staff development;
  —operational control;
  —planning;
  —commercial awareness.

Such lists can be helpful but need to be carefully applied. Their use can lead to an over-inclusive wish list of characteristics which, if accepted, could result in an unwieldy psychometric battery. In fact where characteristics are poorly specified there is a temptation to fall back on seeking to measure experience.

What we mean by competencies

The competency movement, emerging since the late 1980s, has done much already, and seems set fair to do much more to clarify thinking about requisite behaviours and hence the appropriate psychometric measures to predict them. However, the movement itself has sometimes got bogged down in what appears to be over-specification.

A number of definitions of competency have been produced. In my view the most effective, due to Evarts (1987), is the following: 'A competency is an underlying characteristic causally related to effective or superior performance on the job.'

The last part of the definition tells us where we are in terms of why the competency is of interest and focuses us on the end result. Causally related means that we are concerned with what is relevant for a particular job. A competency such as creativity would be relevant for a graphic designer but probably not for an actuary or a mortician. The specification of the characteristic as underlying means that we are not just concerned here with superficialities. Neither the wearing of a beard nor the possession of a particular qualification, though sometimes passionately cited in terms of their relevance to success or lack of success in a job, would be admitted into the ranks of competencies!

Competency descriptions

Competencies are often grouped into categories such as individual or information handling with a short descriptive title, a defining subtitle, a paragraph of text and a range of positive or negative indicators, as in the example below.

Managerial Competency Example
INDIVIDUAL
Control of Initiatives
Making decisions and taking charge of events

The executive strong in control of initiatives makes a definite decision to proceed with an action or actions. They see themselves as owners of decisions and the actions required to stem from them. They may position a variety of others in representative or supportive roles, for instance using inputs from financial or marketing deputies, but they will be clear that it is themselves who are setting actions in train. They may see their work as a series of projects to be set in motion. They will take initiatives not only in terms of making things happen, but also in the sense of self-management. They will be in control of their own time as a resource and will have distinct means of coping with the stresses of the job. They will be prepared to follow through tenaciously, not letting problems deter them and not succumbing to hostility.

POSITIVE INDICATORS	NEGATIVE INDICATORS
Can identify when a decision to proceed was taken.	Vague about decision points.
Takes charge of a range of activities – calling meetings, briefings, initiatives, planning.	Lets activities 'take their course'.
In charge of their own time.	Event driven.
Statements indicating ownership personally or with or through immediate group.	Ownership for actions resting with outsiders, may be vague 'they'.

(Reproduced with permission of MSL Human Resource Consulting Limited.)

Sometimes, rather than positive and negative indicators there may be a scale of indicators as in the second example below, which is a competency definition for a distribution company undergoing reorganisation.

FLEXIBILITY

The ability to modify one's approach to achieve a specific outcome and to maintain effectiveness during changes in distributive operations.

Flexibility has two distinct components which the effective team member understands he or she must display.

The first component is about flexibility of approach, which requires changes in personal style or methods to achieve a particular outcome. The effective team member understands the need to behave differently in different circumstances or with different people, for instance distinguishing between head office clerical staff and people in the depots.

The second component is about maintaining effectiveness during change, that is adapting to changing situations over a period of time, for example, coping with the introduction of new vehicles or shift rotas.

PERFORMANCE INDICATORS

Over the top: Does not know own mind, 'wishy-washy'.
Tends to adopt the last course of action suggested.

Positive: Adaptable, flexible, versatile.
Tries out an approach, but if it appears not to be working switches to other methods. If objectives change, is able to change behaviour to suit. Prepared to learn new skills and new tasks. Willing to cover for colleagues.

Negative: Inflexible, seldom compromises.
Inclined to persist with original line of action beyond point when it is evident to others that it will not succeed. Expresses disquiet if objectives change. Reluctant to undertake other people's tasks.

Missing: Totally rigid behaviour.
One approach to all situations. Will not discuss alternative approaches. May persist in set path, even when directed to do otherwise.

(Reproduced with permission of MSL Human Resource Consulting Limited.)

Deriving competencies

The derivation of competencies typically represents a substantial effort involving quite sophisticated research methods such as repertory grid, as discussed in Chapter 7. As such they are a considerable advance on the characteristics checklist discussed above. Such definitions, like their counterparts in more traditional job definitions, are increasingly used to give quite distinct indications as to appropriate psychometric methods.

Competencies have also been used to specify standards in relation to training – a method, in fact, foreshadowed over 20 years ago in the systems approach to training utilised by the Royal Air Force. This approach for the first time specified training outcomes in terms of what was actually required to be done, rather than in terms of a pass mark in an end of course exam. Consideration was given to issues such as, 'If trainee fitter Smith gets 60 per cent in an exam, what is the impact of the 40 per cent he does not know on the airworthiness of the aircraft he is servicing?' It was such thinking that led to the realisation of the need for the concentrated, behavioural approach represented in the competencies movement itself.

In the UK this movement received a point of focus in 1988 with the establishment of the Management Charter Initiative (MCI). Originally set up as the marketing arm of the National Forum for Management Education and Development, this body is progressively defining national standards of competence for managers at different levels. To date standards have been developed for supervisors, first line and middle managers with those for senior managers now (1994) in course of development. The standards are structured in a cascaded fashion from purpose, through roles and units of competence to elements and performance criteria. Finally range statements/indicators show the situations in which competent performance is desired.

This scheme offers a great deal of specificity and indeed may sometimes indicate greater detail than will have been entertained by an intending user. At the time of writing such issues are ongoing matters of debate.

The way ahead

Altogether, the thinking about and use of competency definitions appears to be a sound way forward in relation to considering candidates' fitness for jobs, and in specifying appropriate psychometric techniques. In the next chapter we shall review a series of selection situations and broadly how psychometric testing may be applied in each of them. Before doing so the reader may like to consider the case of the Acme Engineering and Plastics Company set out below.

THE ACME ENGINEERING AND PLASTICS COMPANY –
EPISODE 1

Tom Evans, site manager of the Acme Engineering and Plastics Company's main plant and office complex in Welchester, sat at his desk in the firm's 'mahogany row'. He was waiting for a meeting with Will Stevens, the company's new young personnel manager.

As he waited Evans mused. They were getting together to discuss the recruitment of a new administration manager for the site. There seemed such a lot of fuss about these things today. On the phone Stevens had muttered something about 'profiles' and 'psychometrics'. He said he thought it was important that they worked on a competency description for the job. In the old days Tom had had one of the senior secretaries ring round a few agencies and ask for some suitable people. If there was a need to put an ad in the paper he would usually write the copy himself and he would get one of the draughtsmen to do a line drawing of the factory.

He usually had a good idea of the type of person he wanted. An administrator obviously had to be experienced. That had seemed to be one of the major appeals of the previous incumbent. You would think somebody who had been a company secretary with a chemical subsidiary of one of the big oil companies would have been able to cope quite well with the work at Acme. Still the fellow had never seemed to want to get involved in any of the real details and although he had known before he joined that his department was only three people he seemed to expect them to carry out everything themselves.

Of course you could not have a youngster in a position like this one. He was going to have to interface with the senior management and board further down the corridor on the one hand, and also be able to deal with the engineering department managers and shopfloor supervisors. All of them were pretty long in the tooth. But he didn't want somebody who was just waiting for his pension either. There were things to be done and someone with some new ideas who would still have a feel for the way in which a traditional firm like Acme wanted to work would probably be best. So probably no more than 50 and no younger than, say, 44. Of course he must have good administrative experience and maybe an administrative qualification. Perhaps going for an ex company secretary had been a bit too high flying, even though the chap had seemed happy to take the salary.

He had heard that some of these tests could tell how a person fitted in. He really was not sure how that could possibly work. Maybe he ought to put something about flexibility in the ad. They had had some trouble hadn't they with the administrative supervisor before last, the senior position reporting into the managerial post. He remembered how the whole place had gone into overdrive when they had received a large export order with a very short turnround period. Administration needed to throw themselves into supporting the commercial department in a whole range of things, including shipping arrangements behind the Iron Curtain. Then they found themselves involved in translation and printing of the necessary brochures. He smiled ruefully again. Geoff had said that he had not seen it as part of his job to do that and he wasn't going to miss his kendo class two weeks running. Still, perhaps the right manager could have handled it better. You really did sometimes need a person who could combine firmness and tact.

Then there was the new computer system to get to grips with. Naturally it was accounts-driven but administration had to understand what it could do for them. The last chap had never seemed to comprehend how the production spreadsheets would be part of his concern. Probably a bit slow on the uptake on the numbers side thought Evans. Funny, he had never considered asking him about that. He prided himself, of course, on the way his engineering training had always helped him in his own work. Better have someone with some solid numerical background to his education: an A level in maths or maybe even sticking out for a graduate in one of the more analytical subjects. He would have to be careful he didn't end up with an accountant though. He'd never found one of them that didn't get on his nerves after a while, too pernickety – a lot of them were. In this type of operation there is detail and detail. You needed to know what was important and then follow that through hard, but not chase every last figure through to the ultimate limit.

He was beginning to feel depressed talking to himself like this when Stevens finally walked in.

'Good afternoon Tom', he said. 'I've been thinking about your administration manager post and I have brought the old job description from the file. I think it will give us some clues as to the type of person we want but a lot of it is a bit vague. However, you seem to have some ideas yourself from what you said on the phone, even though there may be one or two question marks in your mind. I have drawn up a preliminary list of characteristics. You'll see that I've indicated flexibility, a rapid learning style and numerical reasoning. We could probably cover that in a personality questionnaire and one of the standard ability tests. By the way the old JD referred to graduate qualifications, but I can't quite see why.

'There was also a quaint reference to institutional professional membership, without any clarity about which professional body was concerned. There doesn't seem to be any legal requirement of that nature, so I propose to ignore it. There is also a reference to 20 years' commercial business experience, preferably in a manufacturing environment. I think if we're placing an advertisement we might indicate a liking for working in the manufacturing sector but, of course, for the right person who fits the requirements in terms of behaviour it doesn't matter much if he has got 20 years' or 20 weeks' experience and of course the same applies to age . . .'

Evans wasn't quite sure yet whether his day was improving or not. Could this fellow have the answers?

SUMMARY

- The specification of information flows in selection is rarely clear.

- Models used are often implicit rather than explicit.

- The use of experience and age and over-reliance on conventional interviews may be based on mistaken views as to their contribution and effectiveness. Much of the ground intended to be covered by such means may, in fact, be better addressed by psychometrics.

- Job definitions will aid the specification of required characteristics in ways amenable to psychometric testing.

- Competencies can provide a high degree of precision in specifying what is relevant and so help decide what particular psychometric tests should best be used.

4

Tests and selection: the practice

In this chapter we look at some broad types of selection situation, from high volumes sourced externally to cases of internal selection. In conjunction with these areas we consider a number of issues of general relevance in psychometric applications, including cut-off scores, and the interplay between tests and other procedures.

LARGE VOLUME RECRUITMENT APPLICATIONS

Where large numbers of individuals need to be recruited into a company at any one time it is common for ability or aptitude tests to be applied either singly, in pairs or in whole batteries. In these situations personality testing would usually be excluded at the initial stage, because of the necessary complexity of interpretation. Examples of large volume recruitment roles include graduate entry schemes, retail management and sales staff, and financial consultants in the insurance industry. Relocation of offices or opening of new factories also often occasion high volume recruitment.

Use of norms

The very idea of large scale recruitment raises the possibility of scope for local (that is specific to the recruiting organisation) validity studies to be conducted. Where this is so the results of such studies can be used to determine where cut-offs on the test or tests should best be placed. In practice such specific studies will only rarely have been carried out in advance of establishing the need to recruit. By that time there is rarely the time available – and not usually the money either – to undertake such a study. One is then obliged to rely on a set of norms developed elsewhere. As discussed in Chapter 2 the norms available may be general population or drawn from a similar occupational group to the target. (For example, in one recruitment application current at the time of writing I have been able to recommend the use of a norm table for clerical staff in financial services when recruiting clerical staff for a financial services company!)

The strength of relationship

If the test has some validity then there will be a positive degree of relationship between performance on the test and performance in the job. In a perfect relationship if each individual's score on the test were plotted against his performance in the job all the points would lie in a straight line as in Figure 4.1. In practice, of course, such relationships are not found. They would, in fact, be the equivalent of being able to translate inches to centimetres or pounds to kilogrammes.

Where tests are positive predictors then in general those scoring higher on the test perform better in the job. In such cases plots linking test scores and performance for individuals are scattered within a roughly elliptical shape, such as that illustrated in Figure 4.2. While in general a higher test score is associated with higher performance, there are some individuals who do not perform very well in the job despite having a high test score and conversely some with a lower test score whose job performance would be effective.

The closer the clustering of points around the straight line the more effective the test will be in predicting performance. As prediction becomes less and less effective the more the boundary in which the individual plots fall moves outwards, bulging the ellipse. The ultimate is where there is no relation whatsoever between the test and performance on the job. Then, for any test score, any level of performance is as likely as any other. The distribution of individuals when test score and performance are plotted together is then bounded not by an ellipse but by a rectangle (see Figure 4.3 on page 80).

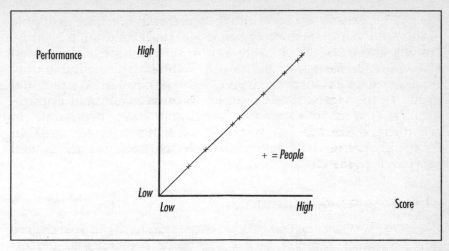

Figure 4.1 *The perfect test - performance predicted with certainty*

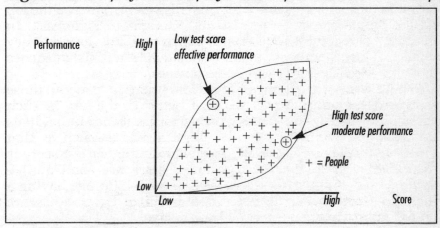

Figure 4.2 *A positive predicator - but some errors*

The correlation coefficient

These relationships are captured statistically in the concept of *correlation* and expressed in the correlation coefficient r. This is a number ranging from +1 down to −1. An r of +1 would result from the straight line relationship as shown in Figure 4.1. Figure 4.3, with the distribution showing no relationship would give us an r of zero. For a perfect negative relationship with an r of −1, scores on one dimension would diminish with perfect

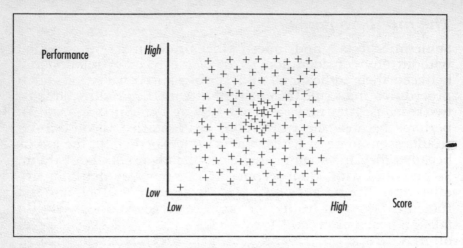

Figure 4.3 *The pointless test - no predictive power*

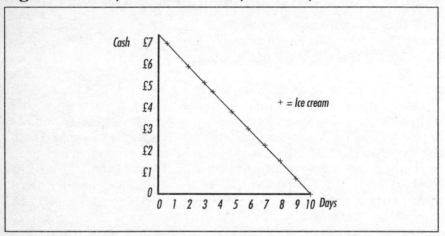

Figure 4.4 *Perfect negative correlation - the effects of ice-cream purchasing upon cash*

predictability as those on the other increased. This is shown in Figure 4.4. This could be illustrated by the careful schoolboy with £7 holiday pocket money, spending it at the rate of 70p per day to furnish himself with one ice-cream per day throughout his ten-day trip to the seaside. The correlation coefficient is an important expression to which we will return at various points throughout the book (see also Appendix 1).

The numbers game

Sometimes tests – and indeed other procedures – are applied without any consideration at all of the form of relationship between their indications and performance on the job. Such procedures may still have a certain superficial attraction for two reasons. They may seem to be giving some further insights, perhaps because the words that are produced in describing results seem to tie in with what is understood about the job or because they have some cachet of the rigorous about them. Second, and with equal scepticism, one may say that they are often attractive because they provide a means – albeit one not rooted in any real truth – of making decisions about who to take on board or process further. Thus if there is a score a cut-off may be applied to it and there will, therefore, be a means of making a decision and spending any further investigative time on a smaller group than those originally considered.

If the relationship between the test measure and performance on the job is random then the use of the procedure will have added no other value whatsoever than that of reducing the number of candidates to be processed in a way that could have been achieved by tossing a coin.

This simple fact is illustrated further in Figure 4.5. This indicates the situation where (a) there is no relationship between the score on the test measure and performance on the job, and (b) it is possible to think of performance on the job in relation to success or failure. It can be seen that as the cut-off level on the test is shifted from level 1 to level 2 the proportion of those succeeding and those failing remains constant even though, of course, the numbers change. It is the numbers changing that gives the spurious impression that something useful is happening.

For many jobs, of course, the dividing line between successful and unsuccessful performance will be blurred. However, there are situations, for instance those involving training whether it be for, say, a heavy goods vehicle driver or for an accountancy qualification where a more distinct line of success will be indicated.

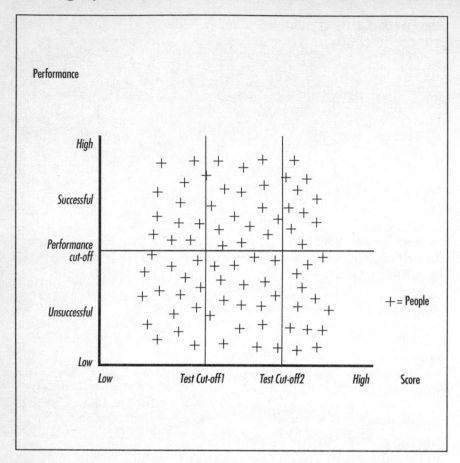

Figure 4.5 *A pointless exercise - applying test cut-offs to tests with zero correlation with performance*

False positives and false negatives

The extreme case of zero correlation is, perhaps, relatively rare and the practical picture is complicated by a number of other issues. Consider now a case such as that shown in Figure 4.6. In this situation the test is a rather poor predictor of success but there is still some degree of relationship. Thus, on the whole, those with a higher score tend to do better on the job than those with a lower score, but there are many discrepancies. If, again, a cut-off is applied to the test score then it will be found that those taken on will tend to do better than if those with scores below the cut-off had been taken on or if people had been chosen at random. Thus the test has some value to add.

Of course a poor predictor means that some mistakes will be made. There will be some false positives or false selections and some false negatives or false rejections. That is, there will be some individuals achieving above the test cut-off who will not succeed in the job. There will also be a number of those below the cut-off, who were rejected but who could have done the job perfectly effectively. However, the proportion of these will be smaller than the proportion correctly selected and correctly rejected. The more the shape tends towards the straight line relationship, as in Figure 4.7, the smaller the proportion of the false positives and false negatives.

Leveraging the weak predictor

Note, though, that providing there is a positive correlation then, other things being equal, the highest possible cut-off is desirable. It is doubtless this that employers grope towards when they set higher academic standards. The relationship between such standards and performance in a job may be slight, but if it is present at all then the chances of a successful job outcome by hiring those with, say, first-class degrees rather than those with second-class degrees is evident. However marketplaces are dynamic; first-degree candidates know their market worth and may well require higher salaries, complicating the picture further. A better procedure might well be to seek to introduce a higher degree of prediction by substituting a test procedure for the academic standard!

The question of cost also emerges within the testing field as such. More, better research to better define competencies or to refine and tailor the test procedures rather than take them off the shelf, will all tend to shift the shape of the relationship between the test and job success closer to the straight line ($r = 1$), making it more like the safe task of estimating centimetres from inches. However such work clearly takes time and money, and even a relatively weak predictor can be leveraged further.

Figure 4.8 shows a case when cut-offs are set progressively higher still with the same relatively poor test predictor. The proportion of unsuccessful selections progressively diminishes and the proportion of the successful increases. Of course, at the same time the absolute number of people taken on board at all

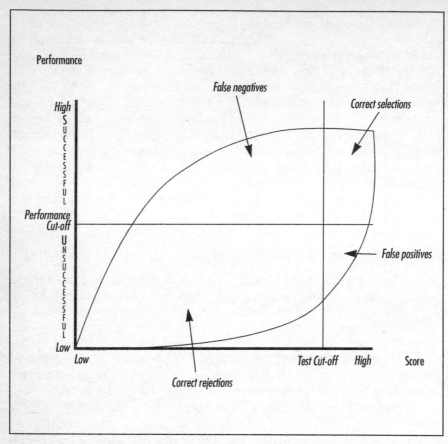

Figure 4.6 *Applying a cut-off to a weakly predictive test*

and the absolute number of successful ones also reduces. Therefore, for such a system to yield sufficient numbers the pool of applicants needs to be extended. The proportion of people tested who are selected is known as the *selection ratio*. If the pool of applicants can be extended then the selection ratio can be kept low and only the best appointed.

To increase correlation or candidate numbers?

If we consider what is implied by all of this we can see that there may be two broad options to think about. The first is to increase the predictive accuracy of the test, which requires

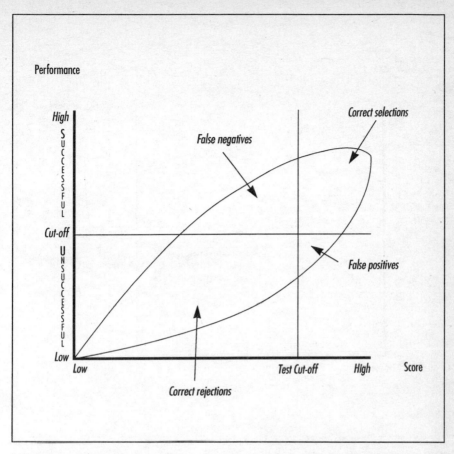

Figure 4.7 *Applying a cut-off to a strongly predictive test*

investment. The second is to increase the pool of applicants, which also implies expenditure in capturing and/or processing of them. Which approach to adopt will vary with circumstances.

Attempts to state the relationships among the different issues and variables involved have been going on for many years. For example, over 50 years ago Taylor and Russell (1939) devised tables linking expected successes for different levels of correlation, taking into account numbers of successful performers found without the use of tests. Later treatments of the same issues have tended to regard such early attempts at cost benefit

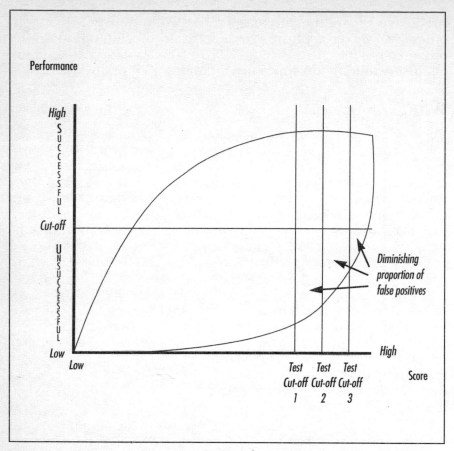

Figure 4.8 *Effects of various cut-offs with a weakly predictive test*

evaluations as primitive, but still fail to give really comprehensive guidance.

Increasing a pool of applicants will lead to more rejected and hence disappointed candidates, and if the relationship between test score and performance is very weak could lead to an increased likelihood of discrimination in some cases (this will be returned to in more detail in Chapter 6). Such issues are not usually addressed in the same breath as the hard-nosed cost benefit analyses (see for example, Jones in Toplis et al 1987).

On the whole my recommendation would be to opt for methods likely to give some increased accuracy in prediction. Sometimes the time, money and effort spent in improving predictive capability can be borrowed from that which might otherwise go on arbitrary or inaccurate procedures at some other stages of the process. It will always tend to militate against candidate disappointment and risk of prosecution.

What comes next?

Very often, of course, the psychometric procedures in mass selection are set in a chain of activities. Sometimes this chain involves a further review, after the psychometric testing of candidates falling just below the cut-off. This is not altogether unreasonable. It is evident from consideration of the dynamics of the processes as explained above, that any test is an imperfect predictor and that there will be some people below the cut-off who will, in fact, have a chance of succeeding, (quite a lot of people in a case such as that shown in Figure 4.8).

The wisdom and likely success of such a way of proceeding will depend on several factors though. First there is the question of how far below the original cut-off should be regarded as just below and second the procedures used for the further investigations. If the revised or provisional level below the original cut-off is very close to the original so that a relatively narrow band of scores is yielded for further consideration, then the overall chance of success would be not much different from that with the higher level cut-off. (Of course this also implies that not many more individuals will be considered.) As the cut-off is shifted further and further away, although the number of potential successful applicants increases, so does the number and the proportion of the unsuccessful. At the ultimate such a proceeding amounts to abandonment of the test altogether.

Another statistic: the standard error

Just what constitutes a narrow band of revision of scores does not have to be regarded arbitrarily. Reference can be made to the *standard error of measurement*. Derived from the reliability studies on the test and typically reported in test manuals, the standard error indicates the expected range of variability of a test score. If it is relatively large then the true test score can be expected to lie in a wider range than if it is narrow. Hence, with a large standard error relatively large shifts in the cut-off score could be regarded as still within the original basis of decision.

(Standard errors are discussed further in Appendix 1.)

Let us consider now the further review of candidates in the provisional band below the original cut-off score. If the procedure now to be applied is arbitrary and itself not a predictor at all or a very weak predictor, then this amounts to a random choice among that next group considered, in effect making a pretence of a systematic approach to selection for this group. On the other hand, if this group is now subjected to a more accurate process, there will still be a cost but the overall accuracy of selection would have been enhanced.

It is now time to look in again on the further tribulations of the Acme Engineering and Plastics Company, as set out below.

THE ACME ENGINEERING AND PLASTICS COMPANY – EPISODE 2

Will Stevens was faced with a problem. The recruitment programme for computer programming staff for the company's administration centre was just not getting enough people through. The programme had been set up prior to Will's arrival and the arrangements were sufficiently far advanced, that after a brief check on what was to be done he decided to let it run.

The young personnel officer there had been an enthusiast for psychometrics and had introduced a test from a well-known publisher involving logical reasoning, numerical calculations and flow diagramming skills. Hardly anybody seemed to be getting through it. The personnel officer wondered if the original cut-off set had been too high. He had sent Will some figures which suggested that if they lowered the acceptable score by 2 points they would get an extra 20 per cent of people through.

Will decided it was time to take a closer look. He unlocked a filing cabinet and took out his test manual.

Multiple testing

So far in this chapter we have considered only the case of a single test with a single cut-off to be taken into account at any one time. But what of the case when several different tests are used, either completely separate ones or forming part of a battery? In the latter case, for instance, with batteries such as the *Differential Aptitude Test* (*DAT*, referred to in Chapter 1); or the *General Ability Test* (*GAT*) which comprises separate verbal, non-verbal numerical and spatial tests, there is usually the advantage of a common set of norms for the whole battery. This gives some basis for comparisons among the different tests used. If tests are drawn from different sources then the norms available will often reflect widely differing samples, limiting the scope either to combine or trade off scores.

Combining test scores

When there is scope to do the necessary research, test scores can be combined to give a weighted sum, in what is known as a *multiple regression equation*.

Such an equation gives a direct readout of predicted performance. This approach is attractive and in one sense ideal; test scores are put in and performance on the job comes out! In practice life is not so simple. There is, of course, the problem of the criterion of performance discussed in Chapter 1, which multiple regression shares with other means of interpretation of test scores. (As suggested earlier in this chapter this is, in effect, side-stepped by making comparisons on a normative basis.) There is then the question, again mentioned before, of gaining adequate data for research. It is usually just not a practical proposition to do this in conjunction with a selection or recruitment programme and so one often relies on off-line studies reported in the test manuals or research literature.

Again the apparent simplicity of the idea of combining weighted scores can be questioned. Inherent in it is the idea that a high score on one test can offset a low score on another. Although this may be so in general, it may gloss over the negative impact of very low scores. For example, a battery used for clerical selection might include a clerical checking test (with items such as shown in Figure 2.2). Someone scoring very low on such a test might be so inaccurate that all their work would have to be checked and in effect reworked. High performance in other aspects of their work, as predicted by other tests in the battery would not compensate. The multiple regression approach would tend to mask the impossibility of adequate compensation for the area of limitation.

Another approach to the use of multiple test scores is the use of multiple cut-offs. A minimum score is decided on each of the tests, so that only those above each of these minima is considered further. Sometimes further consideration is in terms of another process entirely and sometimes it is in terms of, in effect, combining scores. Thus a score level averaged over the various tests is sometimes set. Without specific research there will be a degree of arbitrariness about any of these approaches to multiple tests, with the existence of relevant norms often the firmest foundation available. (For some further comment on multiple regression and multiple cut-offs see Appendix 1.) It is also worth noting in this correction that considerable management effort may be required in working with someone whose profile of characteristics is made up of extremes. One needs in such cases to be constantly considering whether enough support is being given to cover the areas of relative deficit, and if enough leeway is being provided for the strengths to have full scope to demonstrate themselves. Managing someone with a more consistently average profile is likely to be a less demanding if also less exciting proposition.

Some guidelines

Overall the guidance to intending recruiters here will be as follows.

- Consider competencies and choose tests accordingly. If there is insufficient information to do this do not just launch into a recruitment advertising campaign and arbitrary test procedures, but be prepared to spend more time in researching and building some form of competency description.

- Consider the numbers of people that you are prepared to process and organise your procedures accordingly. (In many situations precise numbers will be difficult to gauge but if you are overflowing with candidates you will be tempted to apply more or less arbitrary procedures rather than using effective psychometric methods.)

- Consider cut-offs and if you are tempted to lower or to raise them think about whether this amounts to degrading or enhancing your original testing process.

ONE-OFF AND SHORTLIST ASSESSMENT

Consultant's reports

In many circumstances psychometric tests are applied in occasional rather than large scale applications. This may happen, for example, for middle or senior management posts, or in relation to the replacement of key functional staff. Again the existence or creation of job definitions or, better still, competency models and the avoidance of arbitrary selection on the basis of irrelevant or very weak predictors such as age and educational qualifications is to be encouraged.

Sometimes the use of psychometrics in these circumstances takes the form of reference to an internal or more often external consultant in effect with a view to finding out things that have not been thrown up in earlier procedures. These would often have consisted of sifting of CVs and the use of interviews, both of which relate largely to experience. In such cases there is a recognition that psychometric procedures may save the costs of expensive hiring mistakes which could have a negative impact on the hiring organisation in general and particularly on the hiring executive. Giving clues to the most appropriate way of managing the candidate, if hired, can also help optimise his contribution.

Sometimes in these cases the competency requirements may not be made as explicit as elsewhere, particularly in the case of an external reference to a consultant who may use a more or less standard battery, often including a fairly broadband personality questionnaire. (The idea that there may be something else to find out about the candidate reflects an implicit appreciation of the fact that the procedures likely to have been used earlier - even though an enormous amount of time and money may have been spent up to this point - are, in effect, weak predictors!)

The potential interaction and support between personality and ability tests such as those measuring high level reasoning can also be seen as coming into play here. A relaxed individual may not in general feel stressed by high workloads but, if his cognitive reasoning abilities are weak he may still fail to cope effectively. Conversely, a more tense person with a high reasoning capacity may be able to cope more effectively. A sample consultant's report weighing up the information from a short battery of this nature follows.

A REPORT ON JOHN JONES, MANAGERIAL CANDIDATE FOR COMPANY Z

BRIEF DESCRIPTION OF TESTS AND QUESTIONNAIRES USED

1. Tests of Reasoning Ability

Two tests from the Graduate and Managerial Assessment Series have been used to assess the level of intellectual effectiveness. The tests measure verbal reasoning and abstract reasoning ability and are designed to discriminate levels of ability among graduate level, managerial candidates. Abstract reasoning skills would indicate an ability to recognise patterns and trends and to be able to switch easily between different contexts and levels of analysis.

Comparisons are made with a norm population of graduate level managers and are expressed in percentile terms.

2. *16 Personality Factor* Questionnaire

This is a well researched and documented questionnaire and provides a comprehensive picture of an individual's basic personality. As the name implies, 16 different and independent personality dimensions are measured. Interpretation of the information focuses on aspects of behaviours known to be closely associated with managerial effectiveness, and in particular the key competencies identified as being significant for this particular post.

FINDINGS

Pattern of Interpersonal Relationships

A strongly goal-oriented individual, he will readily and easily work as part of a team, where he will actively and assertively seek out a leadership role. He displays a need to have control of the circumstances in which he finds himself and while he will be prepared to delegate, he will maintain a high level of vigilance to ensure that progress towards a given objective is maintained.

He is naturally disposed to be open and frank in his communication with others and will prefer to 'get on with the job'. He recognises that this approach does not always agree with others and this is an aspect of his behaviour which he constantly tries to moderate.

He will display a high level of social confidence and quickly be at ease in any work or social situation although he may become impatient in a culture which becomes preoccupied with the means rather than the end.

His social confidence is underpinned by a natural gregariousness and to be effective he will need to have a team around him, in part to act as a sounding board for his ideas but also to be the means of implementing his decisions. He will always initially seek for others to critique his own ideas and arrive at a consensus on a course of action. He will, however, have no compunction in imposing his will if agreement is not readily reached. It is critical that those working for him adopt the same high standards as those which he sets for himself as he is unwilling to 'carry passengers'.

It is interesting to note that while he will display an assertiveness and an independence of mind, his continuing effectiveness will be dependent upon a substantial level of positive feedback and 'stroking'.

Problem Solving/Decision Making

Faced with a decision he will be diligent in seeking out all the pertinent essential information which relates to that particular issue. He will be analytical in endeavouring to understand the causes rather than the phenomena itself and having gained his understanding of the causes will use these to synthesise a solution and decision. When arriving at a decision, it is important that not only should the logic be sound but to use his own words that it should 'smell right'. If a decision does not 'smell right' he is unlikely to go with it and by the same token, if others present to him decisions which do not have the same intuitive appeal, then he will challenge them and press hard for justification.

His problem solving will be typified by a systematic approach and it is improbable that his decisions will break with conventional wisdom. Having arrived at a decision, he will hold to it tenaciously, almost to the point of stubbornness, relinquishing his position only in the face of extremely well reasoned logical argument which must also have an intuitive appeal for him.

Coping With Stress

There is nothing within the profile to suggest that he cannot cope adequately with stresses of operating in a senior position. It is however worthy of note that he may on occasions experience a mild degree of frustration as he gets too close to a particular problem and such frustration will be readily and quickly vented.

Work Style

A natural team player, his optimum contribution will come when he has the opportunity to take the leadership of a team of competent and able subordinates. His particular strength will lie not necessarily in the development of strategy, but rather in the interpretation of strategy into detailed plans of implementation. He will then action this through a relentless drive towards the objectives.

His strength of purpose and striving for achievement demand an environment and culture which puts the realising of objectives above the means of their achievement.

Intellectual Ability

His score on the verbal reasoning test places him on the 15th percentile rank and on the abstract reasoning test at the 25th percentile rank. Allowing for a somewhat disrupted education – his father was a minister of religion and the family moved frequently – I regard the verbal reasoning test as being at a reasonable level. The abstract reasoning score, while not unreasonable, would, however, suggest that his breadth of strategic thought may not be very expansive.

(Reproduced with the permission of MSL Human Resource Consulting Limited.)

Thus such reports set out the various balances in the profile of ability and personality, and can help focus on areas where the candidate may prove to be a liability.

Sometimes the consultant will be briefed very explicitly in terms of the requisite competencies and will shape the report as in the following sample extract.

QUALITY ORIENTATION

A consideration for others and an orientation to service will tend to inform Ms Grey's approach to quality. She also appears to be interested to some degree in understanding people, and will probably make some links between merely operational aspects of training and the change in behaviour or skill that training is intended to bring about.

Her conscientiousness will also underpin quality effectively. However she is not strongly detail conscious and this suggests that under pressure certain aspects of quality might slip on occasions. The significance of this should not be overstressed as we do see her as likely to be well prepared and inclined, for instance, to anticipate any periods of particularly high workload.

The scope for tailoring such reports quite finely to reflect the pattern of likely behaviour in relation to the role means that consultants and their clients will often prefer to work in this way than to use the expert system reports mentioned in Chapter 2. (The use of expert system reports is also discussed in Chapter 6.)

Sometimes there is a temptation to set aside the unpalatable indications that can come out from testing individual candidates. This seems to be the more so, not surprisingly, the more the psychometric procedure is seen as merely confirmatory and, perhaps very particularly, where a number of people in the firm have seen the candidate and felt comfortable with him. Their own observations may be subjective and their conclusions the result of a halo effect – someone judged good in one aspect of relevance, such as assertiveness, is judged good in all. Such circumstances often build up a weight of inertia that can tell heavily against the test findings.

These cases then become equivalent to the procedure of lowering the cut-off discussed above under mass applications. Then the consultant may have to be particularly vociferous or extreme in his comments for any misgivings about a candidate to carry the day. The more closely integrated the testing process is and the clearer the model of requirements against which the consultant is working the more scope there is for an informed comment that is likely to add value to the decision making process. With greater integration there is less likelihood of the psychometric findings just being set aside.

Further exploration – follow-up and feedback

Sometimes testing used for one-off appointments is seen as throwing up ideas for further exploration. It is frankly not clear how useful this process can be. At its best it will, in effect, add to the accuracy of the test process itself, being equivalent to narrowing the distribution of scores ever more closely to the single straight line prediction. A skilled consultant with detailed knowledge of the target role and expertise in the tests used will be able to probe and explore effectively, giving a sound basis for the detailed elaboration of a report and adding considerable value.

At the other extreme, though, the follow-up process may invite substitution of a less accurate measure for one over which considerable care and trouble has been taken – the psychometric test or battery. Consider, for instance, the case in which a candidate going through the *Gordon Personal Profile and Inventory* is described, among other things, as unlikely to invest heavily in personal relations, though having effective superficial sociability. (This would reflect just two of the scales in that instrument.) If the former indication is considered by a panel of interviewers as worthy of further exploration they are more likely, in fact, to be able to gather information relating to the latter characteristic of sociability, concluding that they should set aside the test finding.

A skilled test interpreter is more likely to be able to probe for information at a level which could actually enhance the accuracy of the overall picture. In doing so he or she may, in fact, also undertake feedback to the candidate. Feedback of test results is in general recommended (see, for example, the IPM Code on Psychological Testing 1993).

If integrated into the whole testing and selection process itself feedback can, however, be two-edged. On the one hand discussion with the candidate in which the profile or elements of it are displayed for his comment can elicit illustrative information as just indicated to confirm or refute the test findings. (For example there could be substantial evidence of occasions on which the individual had, in fact, coped with high work levels or high levels of stress if this had been an area of concern.)

Procedures to manage around and cope with areas of difficulty or limitation can also be brought out in this way. For example, I found an otherwise effective senior management candidate with relatively poor numerical reasoning abilities who made use of appropriate subordinates to give him summaries of numerical data in verbal form with appropriate pointers to potential action. Such behavioural evidence could then be seen as adding substantially to the test findings and might not have emerged without explicit feedback in this area. Feedback could also be used to explore how prepared a candidate might be to adopt a tactic such as that just outlined. The person high on the trusting scale of *16PF* might need to exert more control than came most naturally if going into an organisation where laxity had prevailed previously. Exploration of this requirement could help the candidate consider if the job really was for him.

Feedback can, though, also forewarn a candidate, perhaps encouraging him to make an extra effort in a later face-to-face interview situation. For example, someone who would not, by nature of personality, routinely project warmth in the way that might actually be required in a job might still be able to do so for relatively short periods. Similarly, given feedback on a tendency to dominance and over-aggressiveness, this characteristic might be toned down at a later stage of selection.

Clearly care and thought is required in the follow-up questioning and the feedback process. An interesting practical development in the former area, using structured prompt questions is discussed in Chapter 8.

PSYCHOMETRICS AND INTERNAL SELECTION

So far the consideration of psychometric testing in selection has been largely directed towards candidates being recruited and brought on board from outside. Similar considerations will apply to those joining from within an organisation, that is moving from one part of it to another. Hence this section of the chapter is relatively brief. However, there are one or two special factors to be borne in mind.

Don't they know me?

First of all it is sometimes questioned when tests are to be used internally whether that is right and proper. The view is often expressed that 'Surely my company knows me?' or 'Surely I know my people?' or 'I've been around in this organisation a long time; I don't expect to be tested'. These would, of course, be valid arguments if there were data available to provide the information about the individual's suitability for the role. The obvious limitation to begin with here is that one would necessarily be looking at historical performance in a role different from that now being considered, so that there would be likely to be some further dimensions that would require to be explored by one means or another.

The idea of the Peter Principle, by which people are promoted to the level at which they can no longer function effectively is a sad reflection of the fact that previous performance in a different job or one at a lower level is an unreliable guide. Sources that one would think could potentially be tapped such as appraisal data are rarely seen to supply requisite information. Appraisal systems are widely seen as inaccurate, inadequate and/or incomplete. (This state of affairs is, indeed, so prevalent that organisations seem more willing to admit inadequacies in appraisals than in almost any other area of their human resource functioning!)

The idea that a test procedure may be intrusive is, of course, not only confined to internal selection. In the habitual absence of objective data from other sources, such as appraisals, the benefits of psychometric information are evident. It is, of course, by no means uncommon for internal and external candidates to apply and be considered together. In such circumstances the objectivity that a psychometric intervention can bring will help underpin and demonstrate the fairness of the proceeding. In my experience it is about equally common for internal and external candidates both to be a little wary. One group will feel that the insiders might have the advantage of special knowledge, while the others feel that new blood is really being sought. Professionally applied psychometrics can mitigate any such suspicions, as well as actually supplying the objective data required.

Large scale internal applications

Massive selection applications internally are relatively unusual. They may sometimes arise in relation to large scale redundancy situations where those who would otherwise be displaced from the organisation are first given the opportunity to apply for jobs inside. In such circumstances the number of applicants may be large but the number of jobs relatively few. Given the overall emotional climate which will, in any case, attend such circumstances it will be appropriate to proceed carefully. The objectivity of psychometrics is likely to be welcomed. However, it will be important, given the likely small number of vacancies, to shape expectations realistically. Special care may be needed in briefing on the test procedures as such in order to reduce apprehensiveness about what may often be unfamiliar procedures. In these circumstances, too, feedback processes may well need to be linked into other aspects of career counselling that may be undertaken for such individuals.

At this point our discussion moves on to the use of psychometric tests in development, the topic of the next chapter.

SUMMARY

- Ability rather than personality testing is likely to be used in connection with early stages of large scale selection.

- Because specific validity studies may not be practicable cross-reference to most relevant norm groups may often be indicated.

- The degree of relation between test score and performance is expressed in the correlation coefficient.

- Where selection procedures are applied with no consideration for their correlation with success they may give a wholly spurious impression of value.

- Relatively weak predictors can be made to work by setting high cut-offs, but this carries penalties in terms of numbers required to be processed and potential discrimination.

- Psychometric results can, in effect, be degraded by ill-considered shifting of cut-offs or unstructured follow-up procedures.

- Where several tests are used their practical interpretation may involve the use of multiple regression methods or the setting of multiple cut-offs.

- Consultants' narrative reports are often used in relatively low volume selection. For their value to be maximised they need to be integrated into the whole selection process.

- Tests can be used as an effective basis for a further in-depth analysis of an individual, but such analyses are specialised.

- In internal selection psychometric results may often provide information not available from sources supposedly of relevance.

- In recruitment involving a mix of internal and external candidates tests may underpin objectivity and fairness.

5

Tests and development

THE CONTEXT OF DEVELOPMENT

Development for what?

The issue of the use of tests in development raises the question of 'Development for what?' The use of tests in selection will, of course, often have attached to it the idea of a future role, rather than an immediate one. Large oil companies, for instance, take on board groups of graduate trainees and will give them a variety of experiences with the idea of their attaining senior positions at some time in the future. Similar approaches are adopted by the civil service.

In these circumstances, then, the tests used at this initial stage have implications for people being able to pass through the various development stages. However the focus in such cases, as opposed to the use of trainability tests (see Chapter 2) as such, typically seems to be on the future role rather than upon the capacity of the individual to pass through the intermediate development steps. There is a paradox then of identifying competence for a future role, to which someone will progress only after development, but without necessarily making specific links. It is compounded by the fact that organisational structures and roles may change, so that the target role may have altered by the time today's graduate reaches it.

Development in the short term

Apart from graduate entry it is, in fact, more likely that development will be considered at selection with regard to the role under immediate consideration. It is not uncommon, for instance, to find statements in reports following psychometric assessment which relate to such developmental activities, as in the following:

> ... Mr Smith seems likely to focus more upon his own organisation than on creating links outside, as evidenced by a relatively low showing on the team role of 'Resource Investigator'. To succeed to the full as deputy managing director he will need to be effective in representing and marketing the organisation as well as maintaining the necessary operational controls internally. Consideration could be given to the following:
>
> - formal membership of cross-organisational bodies or community based projects;
> - a period shadowing the chairman in his representative capacity;
> - mentoring support from an appropriate non-executive director;
> - attendance on a strategic marketing course.

Such statements beg the question of resources and time available for development and, in fact, the whole context in which development is to take place. Thus, before a test or a set of tests can sensibly be thought about in connection with development, some questions need to be asked and answered. We have briefly considered 'Development for what?'; we next consider 'Development for whom?' Then in the rest of the chapter we shall look at some of the situations in which psychometrics are associated with development, beginning with some specific diagnostic settings and going on to examine the special cases of counselling and development in teams.

Development for whom?

The question here is largely whether development is for the individual being developed or the employing organisation. Many large organisations recognise that it is in their general interest to aid the progress of their people and references to the people employed as their most significant asset are common. Organisations also often understand that a high degree of personal ownership for development will facilitate commitment and be likely to enhance growth of the individual. Sometimes, perhaps as a reaction against bad practices in the past, central functions take individual ownership to a very extreme level. Then local line management may have little awareness of the centrally driven development activities with individuals being encouraged, for instance, to use their personal leave time to take part in development events!

In fact the most balanced view seems to be to regard development as part of a wider career management process in which both employer and employee have legitimate, overlapping but not necessarily identical interests. Within this broader view there is still a need to resolve issues such as who is responsible for bringing development about and who is to be held accountable for it. Both parties – employer and employee – will certainly be stakeholders, working in a mutually dependent way to achieve win-win outcomes.

Ownership and type of test

Because development necessarily involves the individual concerned in personal reflection and understanding, the orientation in testing is likely to be towards those instruments which yield information about, and encourage further deliberation upon personal goals and values. Thus personality questionnaires and interest inventories will be indicated here, and their use will ideally require a substantial degree of support in interpretation. However, the need for support may not be fully understood in advance.

Where development is seen as primarily the prerogative of the employing organisation there will be more emphasis on standardised rather than individually tailored methods with scope, for instance, to feed into common succession planning schemes with associated documentation, as well as aiding individual growth. Personality questionnaires are still likely to be central in such circumstances, but interest inventories, perhaps less so. There may also be a greater focus on ability testing in these cases, although ability testing is certainly not ruled out where ownership of development is seen as resting primarily with the individual.

Some organisations will only have fragmented development activities while others will have integrated systems in which both pathways for development and responsibilities for bringing it about are clearly mapped out. These are likely to include, for example, policy statements about the way in which project or cross-functional responsibilities can be used to aid awareness in certain technical areas and so progress development in that way.

The more the potential facilities and paths for development are specified, the more the psychometric procedures used can be tuned. For example, if training in software skills is a specifically identified option for development in a company, then an information technology aptitude test may be appropriate to see who would be likely to benefit from such training. In practice there is often likely to be a need for a two-way exchange between psychometric testing and development options available: the development procedures help specify the tests and the tests the development procedures.

PSYCHOMETRICS AND DEVELOPMENTAL DIAGNOSIS

The development centre

Special resources and facilities for use in development may include management and other training courses run either internally or external to an organisation. On such courses ability testing is not particularly common, though again there may be use of a number of interest inventories and sometimes personality questionnaires. One special type of development activity and one where psychometric tests are very often used is the development centre.

Development centres are a form of assessment centre, a topic explored in more detail in Chapter 7. Whether the centre is for development or selection, comparable methods of assessment are involved, using a range of worklike exercises which are assessed. In a development centre, as opposed to an assessment centre designed for selection, the results of assessments are much more likely to be regarded as properly owned by the participants or shared between them and the employer. There may also be a further set of exercises and activities, beyond those where performance is evaluated by assessors, which give participants a chance themselves under guidance to explore and evaluate their potential and developmental inclinations.

Psychometrics may be used in connection with the former, assessed exercises or linked in with the latter phase of self-exploration.

In connection with the assessed exercises they will be seen as either providing data to corroborate the findings from the direct observations in the worklike simulations or as giving additional information about competencies and characteristics not readily measured in these exercises. Personality questionnaires will be commonly used, for instance, and outputs from these will include information on interpersonal style. This is likely to be reflected in behaviour used to influence others, which might have been seen elsewhere in exercises involving negotiations. The corroborative nature of information about behaviour from these two sources and the interplay between them can, if sensibly handled, be powerful in helping the participant to understand the impact of that behaviour. For example, a group discussion exercise might have indicated the participant as being forceful, but tending to lose the initiative to others as the discussion progressed. If the *16PF* indicated the same person to be dominant but lacking in warmth, there could be a rationale for an impact that was not sustained. The subsequent feedback might help the person concerned reflect upon whether in real life they sometimes failed to carry initiatives through, because they had failed to build sufficiently strong relationships with colleagues.

Where personality measurement is likely to be able to go further, though, and enter into development as such, is when the personality questionnaire gives indications of areas of support that may be utilised in development to manage around an area of relative weakness. For example, someone indicated as relatively low on dominance but high on persuasiveness might be encouraged to put their persuasive arguments in writing when feasible.

It is in the second stage of self-exploratory exercises that interest inventories such as the *Strong Inventory* referred to in Chapter 2 may be used. Whereas in the first stage of the development centre psychometric tests will be used alongside exercises assessed by others, here they will be operated alongside a variety of other techniques for generating developmental ideas.

One of these techniques is *brainstorming* in which a group of people work together initially to generate suggestions which are first simply captured and listed without evaluation, and then progressively sorted and grouped for inclusion in plans. Another technique is *domain mapping* in which people identify areas of importance in their work and in other aspects of their lives individually, and then indicate the current status of each of these domains in terms and where they would like them to be. Links and tensions between the different domains can then be seen and potentially resolved. An example would be when the absence of an accountancy qualification was seen as hindering career progression, but limited time with a partner tended to preclude attendance at evening classes. The resolution here might be to seek a job providing day release or study leave opportunities for the pursuit of the qualification.

Some of the exercises and activities used here might indeed be seen as intermediate between psychometric procedures such as the interest inventories and the more free format techniques just mentioned. For example, there are questionnaire based methods for exploring personal values, such as Schein's (1985) *Career Anchors*. His approach involves the use of a booklet containing a questionnaire and supporting material for a range of activities, including an interview with a partner. It helps the person define their self-image, values and areas of strength.

Mentoring and executive coaching

Beyond development centres, which are often significant in providing a very concentrated focus on development, there may be a number of other special provisions for development. If mentoring is to be used or if individuals are to be assisted by external coaches then there will be value in such people knowing the outputs of any psychometric procedures that the individuals concerned have undertaken to help diagnose development needs. Such information does have to be used with caution, though. First the question of ownership comes in again and minimally it will be necessary for the person tested to agree to psychometric results being passed on to a third party in this way. In addition, it is important that such a third party should either have undertaken training necessary to under- stand the import of any such results passed on to him or her, or that especial care is given in providing feedback to them.

Sometimes, of course, the third party may, in fact, be skilled in psychometrics, as when a person is referred to an appropriately qualified consultant for a developmental assessment. Such a person is likely to have a range of instruments available to them. The more precise the brief they are given in terms of possible developmental needs and potential development actions, the more finely they can tune their choice of psychometrics.

In many of these types of interventions a range of approaches other than psychometrics as such may be used. They include interrogative methods such as the repertory grid, which is discussed in Chapter 7. Approaches such as Schein's *Career Anchors* referred to earlier in this chapter would also be considered here. So, too, would inventories which, in form, are often close to psychometric instruments, but which may not yet have undergone the rigorous standardisation (see Chapter 6) to qualify as fully-fledged psychometrics. For example, within their *Assessment for Training and Employment* (*ATE*) package (1988a), The Psychological Corporation includes a five-scale inventory designed to help clients deliberate on their occupational preferences. This is not – and is not claimed to be – fully standardised psychometrically, but would appear capable of standardisation. A domain-mapping exercise, on the other hand, would be less amenable to standardisation. Both the inventory and domain-mapping are intended as stimuli to thought, but the former has a readier capability for operating as a measure – as a psychometric procedure.

Repeat procedures

Care is needed if the person concerned is to be placed in the hands of a series of bodies or to undergo a series of events where psychometric procedures may be used. Repeated use of the same personality questionnaires in particular is to be avoided, especially over a short timescale. Repeated exposure with feedback will inevitably lead to contamination and one is likely to see a change in test performance not reflected in behaviour. In other words test validity will be diminished.

Similarly, use of a wide range of measures, developed according to different principles and applied by different people in different contexts is likely just to be bewildering to the person concerned. Thus, although it may be helpful to see someone from the two perspectives of, say, the *Gordon Personal Profile* and the *California Personality Inventory*, the occasional person who turns up with a file of results on five or six different questionnaires may pose the interpreter concerned with quite a challenge in terms of unravelling them. Energy will be spent by him and the individual undertaking the tests in this complex interpretation which might better be used elsewhere and at the end of the day there is danger of confusion rather than enlightenment.

What can psychometrics tell us about what can be developed?

Development implies change and some change may take place in any case as people grow older. (In fact the research findings on this are ambiguous. Some differences in personality scale scores with age have been noted, eg Cattell (1970). However, it is not clear how far such variations are reflected in corresponding behaviour changes. Cronbach (1966) bemoaned the lack of objective records of behaviour which could be used in resolving this issue and the picture has changed little in the intervening years.) It would be possible to see a change in behaviour not reflected in a personality measure as when, say, a shy person manages to develop some techniques to help them project a bolder image. This does happen – it is by no means uncommon in my experience to give feedback to a manager who agrees a personality measure's indications of shyness saying, 'Yes that is the real me, but I have learnt how to hide it and other people do not believe I am shy'.

Utilising what psychometrics tells us about one area of strength to balance up or manage around another area of weakness is a very real and valuable application in development. Psychometrics can also, of course, tell us what is most likely to be the most comfortable and ready path of progress for an individual. Thus, rather than using one set of strengths to help manage a relative weakness an alternative tactic is to develop the person essentially by playing to their strengths. Some management writers have argued this idea strongly. For example Clifton and Nelson, in their book *Soar With Your Strengths* (1992), stress the importance of concentrating almost exclusively upon one's stronger areas and have developed a system of management based entirely upon focusing upon these.

At one level the idea that one should play to strengths is seen as self-evident. The notion of, in effect, taking a master class view of talent and development and concentrating in a hot house atmosphere on the strongest capacities of the strongest individuals has some appeal. At other levels, though, the notion of building on one's strengths is seen as something of a cliché and a way of giving rather woolly encouragement. In fact, the individual looking at their pattern of competencies needs to decide whether to concentrate hardest on strengths, to seek to improve upon relative weaknesses, use strengths to manage weaknesses or team himself with others in a complementary way, using their strengths in support of his or her own weaknesses! (For example, I have frequently advised person- ally disorganised managers to see that they have more organised secretaries.)

The effort for change

Decision making about what to develop and what to manage around may not be straightforward, but psychometric tests can give help by indicating the degree of effort that would be likely to be required to bring about a change of behaviour. One can, in fact, conceive of a hierarchy of ease of change. This ranges from those behaviours based on fundamental beliefs and funda- mental abilities, through those reflecting knowledge and on to the most superficial aspects, for example taking a raincoat when it looks like rain and leaving it at home when it looks as if the weather will be fine. In between the extremes there will be behaviours requiring differing degrees of effort. For example, for a manager to learn how to set up a simple spreadsheet on a PC might require an hour or two of training. If the same manager were poor at making presentations a few days of individual tuition might prove necessary to bring about the desired behavioural change. These ideas are illustrated in Figure 5.1.

When characteristics are more difficult to change then clearly more energy has to be brought to bear to bring the change about, both by the employing organisation and by the individual concerned. Often the attempt will be a failure – the belief is too embedded for anything short of brainwashing to be effective or a gap in, say, numerical reasoning too large even to be made up with daily tuition or else the development methods adopted are insufficiently precise. In the process both the individual concerned and those around him may at worst be

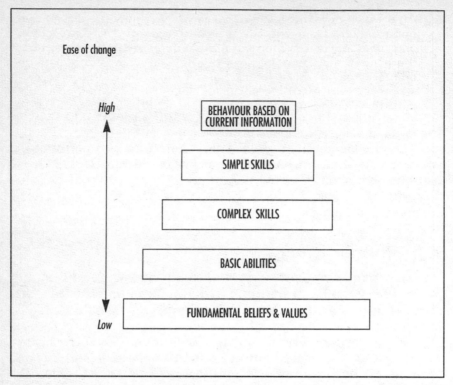

Figure 5.1 *Hierarchy of behaviour change*

severely damaged, and at best be deflected from their most fruitful areas of operation. Consider the following case.

Joe Jones, a middle manager in the central finance function of a large pharmaceutical company, was failing to progress in his career. He was seen as bright, hard-working and committed to the company. Progression would require him to take on substantial man-management responsibilities, looking after one of the function's main accounting production activities.

When he had had people reporting to him in the past things had seemed to go quite well at first, but then always sank into difficulties. Bright youngsters assigned to him seemed to appreciate his expertise and the scope to learn from Joe, but found him negative and difficult to get to know. His management felt a development centre would be a useful next step.

After much demurring and excuses which meant he missed two opportunities he eventually attended a centre. The reasoning and personality psychometric procedures that he undertook there confirmed that he was bright, perfectionistic and fairly uninterested in social interaction. He also indicated in a self-report session that his reason for being in the pharmaceutical industry was to play a part in healing. He had wanted to become a doctor but had not been able to get into medical school. In his position in finance he was frequently appalled at what he saw as unnecessary waste, including the vast range of conferences, promotional events and training activities, such as the development centre itself.

Management decided that he needed some real man-management experience to give him a jolt. With everyone feeling it was make or break as far as the promotion stakes were concerned, he was assigned to the post of deputy director of finance in a small subsidiary. In this position he had wide operational responsibility, including management of the bulk of the finance workforce.

In his first two weeks he had identified some procedural changes which would save the company money and his new director, who had been watching him rather closely, decided to give him a free hand. He duly announced redundancies following the changes he had identified and was surprised when he was criticised for insensitivity in dealing with them.

Two months later, after he and his immediate team had all been working hard to get the year-end figures out, he refused to join them in a small office celebration to note a birthday, commenting that he thought everybody still had work to do, before going back into his office and closing the door ...

Clearly no development of people management skills was happening, and both Joe and his people were being damaged.

In this particular case, although the person concerned was in general in favour of his own development and recognised the need for man-management experience, no one had thought clearly enough about how far he had bought in to the notion of the effort necessary to use the experience offered to him as a development opportunity. In particular, insufficient attention had been given to the implications of the psychometric findings on perfectionism and lack of interest in social interaction, even though these were entirely consonant with his earlier behaviour.

In other cases, though, when full understanding of the psychometric results is combined with a clear commitment to change on the part of the person concerned and tailored developmental activities, there may be substantial shifts in behaviour.

For example, a manager who had been established in an organisation for a long time was having difficulty interacting with a group of new colleagues following a major reorganisation. His personality profile showed coolness rather than warmth and a tendency to favour abstract rather than concrete ideas. Under coaching he learnt some active listening techniques, helping him to tune in better to others. Although he never became effusive his colleagues began to understand that he was interested in them and their ideas, and that he was, in fact, quite keen to help them. Improved listening helped him in his presentation of ideas: he captured the language of his colleagues better and so spoke at what appeared a much more practical level.

At the start of the developmental intervention the manager's intention and commitment were clear: he wanted to get on better with his colleagues and was prepared to work at it.

Attainment and examinations

The use of formalised procedures to measure progress in the course of development is, of course, common in and absolutely essential to the educational process through the use of examinations. In the world of work it is reflected in the use of qualification standards, with varying degrees of closeness to the day-to-day work. For example, the LAUTRO competency guidelines referred to in Chapter 2 can be seen as linked in part to the idea of identifying the degree and form of training required for new recruits. On the other hand examinations in fields such as law and accountancy may be relatively remote from day-to-day practice and the competencies needed to execute them. Law exams do not, in general, address the lawyer's requirement to sell his services for instance. They may have greater affinity with more general ability measures. They are in fact, though, used as tests of attainment – intended to see how far development has progressed.

It is, too, with the field of formal, psychometric, attainment testing that the progress of development can in principle be followed most readily. In practice, though, such tests are far less commonly used in this way than as entry level diagnostic devices. They are then applied to see if the necessary level, say of verbal ability, has already been reached, so that no specific development is seen as required or to determine the form and extent of development necessary. On the other hand, after development activities have been undertaken, their degree of success is more likely to be assessed with an examination or by informal judgement than by a psychometrically prepared attainment test as such.

TESTS IN COUNSELLING

The need for special care

Tests will often be used in a formalised counselling context either in relation to a general initial stock taking or at a significant way point of the process, for instance in order to help establish alternative potential career paths.

Of course, very often the occasion for counselling intervention is some degree of difficulty. It may involve either an individual failing in his work or a redundancy situation, or both. (Comment has already been made in Chapter 4 about the need for very careful briefing when using tests in these cases.) Such circumstances are not conducive to the controlled environment which is an important aspect of test administration (see Chapters 6 and 8 below). Therefore it would not usually be appropriate for psychometric procedures to be undertaken at a very first meeting between the counsellor and the person being tested.

Because development related to counselling may be rather open-ended, this would again point the way to either the broad coverage provided by some personality questionnaires or to wide band ability batteries, or indeed to the scope to choose from a wide range of psychometric instruments. In order to accommodate this range of possibilities the counsellor may need to call on the services of a specialist to select the tests and undertake the necessary interpretation. This may alleviate the need for the counsellor himself to add wide expertise in testing to other skills.

The results of tests used in connection with such interventions are nearly always regarded as the property of the individual and, indeed, the counsellor will ideally establish a clear contract with the person being counselled at the outset. However, within the terms of such a contract it may still be of value for an interpretative report to be made either orally or in writing to the manager of the individual concerned. This may help in order to secure agreement as to an appropriate individualised development path.

In the particular case of a person being made redundant there may, again, need to be drawn a careful balance between the guidance that relates to building upon strengths and that which relates to development in relatively weak areas. The former may be the most affirming and comforting for the person being counselled. However, the latter areas of weaknesses may well have led to poor performance and/or selection for redundancy, and so some degree of care and sensitivity around them will be appropriate. In such cases the individual concerned could be further disorientated through seeking to revamp his behaviour dramatically. Detailed, in effect clinical, consideration of the pattern of psychometric results in the context of the total situation in which the person finds himself will be necessary.

It is also worth noting that the evidence on general personality characteristics of those made redundant is not entirely clear. For example, Brindle (1992) reports research results suggesting that capable executives who undersell themselves lose their jobs rather than those who are high profile, talented irritants, which had been an earlier view. Of course such disagreement over average findings simply serves to underline the need in such cases to proceed on an entirely individualised basis. This view is consistent with what is described as the reality oriented model of redundancy counselling (Prior 1991), whereby confidence is built through a careful and rational stock-taking in which achievements, strengths and weaknesses, and realistic objectives for the future are identified.

The unlocking process

Sometimes the psychometric assessment – particularly one using a personality questionnaire – will help to unlock the counsellor's understanding of the person being counselled. What could otherwise take a lot of painstaking discussion involving progressive removal of defences and barriers can become almost instantly transparent. The following case may illustrate this.

I had a young woman referred to me for counselling after her general performance at work had deteriorated. In particular her morning arrival time had become very erratic.

This behaviour had arisen suddenly and the manager who had referred her for counselling had previously found her to be hard-working and helpful. However, he was aware that a similar episode of late arrival had characterised her behaviour in an earlier position in the same company. The first counselling sessions did not take the situation very far. The woman indicated that she was beginning to find the work less interesting and that this had coincided with a disturbed sleeping pattern. Discussion about future career possibilities failed to advance matters very much.

At the next meeting the idea of a personality measure was introduced, to which she readily agreed. The *Gordon Personal Profile – Inventory (GPP-I)* was used. Two of its scales are responsibility and personal relations. She scored relatively low on the former and very high on the latter. During feedback she indicated that she had fallen out with a flatmate. This was upsetting her and causing the disturbance to her sleep. She felt she *owed it to herself*, to catch up and hence did not always manage to get up on time. For someone as high as she was on personal relations the difficulty with the flatmate was very significant. Responsible behaviour was, in her, in general very vulnerable to the effect of this stress and erratic arrival time resulted. The fact that the erratic arrival at work had not been experienced previously by her present manager appeared to reflect her feeling that she had a good relationship with him and that she valued that relationship. In fact her interest in her work as such had remained at the same level, but she had felt that expressing diminished interest was more plausible and even more acceptable to the counsellor, giving him the idea of a new role for her as something on which to focus.

In her *previous* role, when the late arrival had first been noticed, she had not got on well with her colleagues. Joining a busy office of two older women who were well established she had felt isolated and ostracised, and unable to build the personal relations that were so important to her in all aspects of her life.

Counselling then progressed to rebuild the instrumental link between responsible behaviour and good personal relations, which she had been practising in between the two lapses.

DEVELOPMENT IN THE TEAM

Team roles

Psychometric procedures can also be used in helping organisations think about the development of teams rather than just individuals. The work of Belbin (1981) has given substantial currency to the idea of roles within a team. He distinguished, for example, among the *shaper*, the person giving strong, radical direction or focus, the *coordinator* or *chairman*, and the *teamworker* maintaining climate and good feeling.

Personality psychometrics including *16PF* and *OPQ* can be used to produce indications of individual strengths in terms of each of these team roles. Cumulatively they can indicate the degree of balance or otherwise within a team. For example, a team found to comprise only shapers will be unlikely to agree on objectives or come to any common way of tackling a task. It will, in fact, tend to function as a group of individuals, if indeed it functions at all. The development possibilities for such a group might be, then, centred critically upon importing and/or exporting team members.

The consideration of preset team roles as such is not, though, the only way in which team development may be indicated. Figure 5.2 shows a fictitious scatterplot of personality characteristics for a management team taken from the *16PF* test. Such a team would be unlikely to gell quickly with its members being rigid, rather anxious and not especially outgoing, and might require the use of interactive team building activities. Comfort with one another might not arise naturally in the workplace without such an intervention.

One could also indicate the way in which this particular team could realistically be developed through the addition of other members and their required pattern of competencies as revealed by the psychometrics. As with individual development, very large gaps are difficult to close. For example, if a person with a sten 10 rating on the extroversion scale and sten 1 on control were introduced to the team shown in Figure 5.2 that person would be likely to be disregarded by the remaining team members. A couple of people at, say, sten 7 on extroversion, lower than the present team on anxiety but otherwise similar, would be more acceptable and could progressively help it to develop a more outward-facing posture.

	STEN									
	1	2	3	4	5	6	7	8	9	10
EXTRAVERSION		*	* *	* * *	*					
ANXIETY				*	*	* *	* *	*		
TOUGH POISE		* *	*	*	* *			*		
INDEPENDENCE	*	* *		* *	*	*				
CONTROL						*	* *	* *	* *	*

Figure 5.2 *Scatterplot of 16PF second order sten scores for a management group*

I have also employed the *Myers-Briggs Type Indicator* (*MBTI*) in assigning roles and tasks within a team, so helping the effective development of the team as a whole. In one particular application for an applied research and development team that was just being set up the members were led in a discussion of their individual *MBTI* profiles. They then set up task sub-teams of two in which for instance sensing and intuition were contrasted in the members. These pairs were encouraged to use their different strengths in detail handling (sensing) and overview (intuition) as they tackled the various research tasks.

Unlocking in the team

The unlocking process discussed in relation to individual counselling will often have its equivalent for a team.

A group of managers undertook a psychometric process with the author yielding *Belbin* team role scores. They then discussed the results together. The group leader had high shaper and implementer scores, indicating a tendency both to drive forward to particular end objectives and to involve herself in the execution of tasks to secure these. In the discussion she revealed that she had felt impatience with other group members and considered that she often might as well do the job herself as wait for them. They had found her behaviour perplexing. They had seen her as giving them firm directions on what to do, but when they went to get started she was often half-way to completing the job herself. They had begun to withdraw from involvement with her – which had in turn reinforced her idea that if she wanted something done she had to do it herself.

After the opportunity for clearing the air that the discussion session gave, the manager concerned found herself more uniformly involved in setting direction than carrying out tasks. The other group members felt licensed to remonstrate if she began to do what she had asked them to do.

Studying patterns of individual strengths within the team will also give scope for the appropriate formation of groups to work in mentoring relationships, as the following case may illustrate.

One team with which I was associated discovered in studying a series of psychometric reports that one of their number appeared much stronger in building rapport with his staff than the remainder. As one of the objectives that they had identified for themselves was to achieve better relations with their staff they voluntarily came to the view that studying and seeking to model their behaviour on this individual might help them. Further consideration suggested that the extent to which they would do this would vary depending on their own starting point and so the person strongest in this was also asked to help them further.

He did this by giving them feedback on their behaviour and by some interventions of his own with their staff which helped them directly, and gave his peers a direct rather than a theoretical opportunity to study his behaviour and move towards modelling it.

Although in advance of the discussions about the psychometric results some of them already had positive views of his strengths in this regard, the crystallising factor seemed to be the gap between their own tendencies as revealed by the tests and what had been agreed by all of them as a desirable state of affairs. Thus the psychometric indications provided the impetus for this particular line of development to happen.

POSTSCRIPT ON DEVELOPMENT

In general we can see psychometrics as helping the development process along. The insights they give may provide a spur to action and a means of shaping development to the individual concerned. Such spurs and prompts do seem necessary for many managers. It appears that often the only form of development routinely contemplated for their staff – and seen in the knee jerk form in many appraisal write-ups – is to send people on a training course to fix whatever needs developing. This sheep dip approach tends only to bring about changes in behaviour which will tend to be short-lived.

Some years ago I conducted an internal attitude survey for a major multinational. Attitudes to management were generally favourable, but only a handful of staff endorsed the statement: 'My manager helps me to grow and develop'. The results were so extreme in fact that the first supposition was that they had somehow been entered back to front. They had not. Catalysts bring change about. Psychometric tests can be catalysts in development.

SUMMARY

- Development may be focused on the short term or on future roles. Greater clarity is often needed in defining developmental paths in the latter case.

- Development may be seen as for the good of the individual concerned, the employing organisation or both. Who is seen as owning development has implications for choice of psychometrics and ownership of psychometric outputs.

- Psychometrics are often used in development centres. They may function to complement the assessments made or to facilitate personal deliberations on issues such as preferred development paths.

- In mentoring and coaching, psychometric test results may be valuable, but care needs to be taken to ensure adequate understanding on the part of those receiving them.

- Psychometric tests may help in deciding where developmental effort needs to be expended and in estimating how much effort is required to make a developmental improvement. They may also help decide how an area of weakness might be managed around.

- Apart from attainment tests psychometrics are not readily suited to measuring the progress of development.

- Particular care needs to be exercised when using psychometrics in counselling.

- Insights from testing can help unlock a counselling intervention, by revealing typical patterns of underlying behaviour.

- In team development psychometrics can reveal areas of strength and limitation in the team as a whole, pointing the way for development. Such development might include recruitment of appropriate new team members.

- As in selection, test data need to be interpreted and used with other information and judgement to be of potential use in development.

- Tests can function as catalysts for change and development.

6

Regulation – professional, commercial and legal concerns

BACKGROUND TO REGULATION

The need for regulation

The regulation of psychometric tests has been somewhat chequered in the UK, but now seems to be settling down to a set pattern. There are justifiable concerns that tests that have been poorly prepared can give misleading information. There are also concerns about competence in use of tests including issues such as test choice, administration and interpretation. Some of these matters have been related to ideas of value for money on the part of those purchasing psychometric tests and testing services. There is also the need for those undertaking tests to be treated fairly and with due personal consideration.

These issues have been reflected in a general tightening of standards in the field of training for test use, covering both interpreters of tests and to a lesser extent those charged with their administration. Test publishers have also been concerned to see enforcement of copyright. Not only does this tend to safeguard their commercial interests, it also underpins proper professional usage.

Regulatory concerns in the USA

Many of these concerns have from time to time been focused as a result of litigation, much of it regarding equal opportunities.

In the US in the 1970s equal opportunities cases had reached such a pitch that many organisations abandoned the use of psychometric tests altogether. However there now seems to be a prevalence of wiser counsels suggesting this might have been throwing the baby out with the bathwater, particularly when what was left was a set of unspecified procedures typically defaulting to conventional interviewing.

The peak of the anxiety over testing reflected in the 1970s was not by any means entirely new. Haney (1981) traced a series of social concerns over the use of tests in the US. These ranged from a furore over mental age interpretations of intelligence tests as far back as the 1920s (see also Appendix 1) to worries over the superficiality of multiple choice tests in the 1960s and on to fairness issues in the 1970s. Norvick (1981) traced a shift of focus in the American technical and professional standards for psychometrics. He pointed out that the 1954 standards (APA 1954) were chiefly concerned to see that the test user was provided with enough information by the test publisher to help him in his professional use of the test. Twenty years later (APA et al 1974) the main point of concern had shifted to competency in testing practice such as the obligation on the test user to avoid bias. (The requirement for adequate information still remained.)

The test practitioner as guardian

In the UK today concerns with avoiding bias in testing are evident (see, for example, the paper by Feltham et al 1994, referred to in Chapter 1). So too is consideration of detailed and specific standards of competency in test use.

Of course testing does not take place in a vacuum. The individuals charged with the practicalities of test use in an organisation may not be the same as those with responsibility for associated policy matters. Even such mundane questions as the provision of quiet rooms for testing, secure storage facilities for test materials and results require decisions on resources. The test user must first know what standards are proper and then ensure adherence to them, by education, persuasion and cajoling.

Over the years I have had a number of conversations along the following lines:

'Why can't we just photocopy the stuff?'
'Because it's dishonest, illegal and unprofessional.'
'But no one would ever know.'
'Well supposing I suggested that you should have pirated that new bought-ledger software you've just installed or that we wind back the clocks on all the company vehicles.'
'Oh we couldn't do that it's dishonest ... oh I see what you mean.'

Each of the issues raised will now be addressed in a little more detail. The specific context here, as in the rest of this book, will be that of occupational testing. To that end many of the points made, such as those about qualifications and equal opportunities, are particular to that context. However other comments such as those on copyright are germane to any sphere of psychometric testing.

TEST DESIGN AND CONSTRUCTION

Similar standards apply on both sides of the Atlantic with regard to construction. In the UK the major regulatory body in test use is the BPS, operating through its Steering Committee on Test Standards. The BPS has laid down standards for the design and construction of tests. These are directed first at ensuring adequate validity and reliability, along the lines outlined in Chapter 1. They also involve the standardisation of tests to produce norms. These norms, together with the reliability and validity data, should be presented in a manual. This provides the test user with the necessary data for informed use.

Such standards do not have the direct force of law and, indeed, there is a grey area in relation to the extent to which they are seen as required to be fulfilled by regulatory bodies. Independent and objective review leading to entry in Buros's *Mental Measurement Yearbook* implies adequacy of design without guaranteeing it. The BPS now has its own review publication for ability and aptitude tests, and is in the course of preparing a comparable one for personality questionnaires. It is also evident that the technical merits of some tests may sometimes be matters of dispute. Reference has already been made in Chapter 2 to the debate surrounding normative and ipsative tests in which some well-known British psychologists are involved.

Cook (1992) wrote an article generally critical of the *DISC/ Personal Profile Analysis* – a short personality measure used in salesforce selection. Among other things he referred to limited data in the technical manual for the instrument and cited its absence from the *Mental Measurement Yearbook*. However, the *DISC* instrument continues to have many advocates among sales managers and is widely used. This is not just perversity; in a recent discussion I found a personnel manager recently converted to the *DISC* system, unaware that there had been any question as to its stature as a psychometric instrument.

There are perhaps no absolute guarantees with or without regulation, but competence in test use, to which we now turn and as indicated through appropriate qualification, will help more organisations choose better which tests to use.

COMPETENCE AND QUALIFICATIONS

Background to the BPS scheme

The issue of qualifications in test use has been evolving in the UK in recent years and the present system is, in fact, being introduced a step at a time. (This has produced some anomalies and discontinuities. For example some test users have suddenly found themselves debarred from tests that were previously available to them, because they had not undergone the training that was not in fact in place when the tests concerned were originally developed!)

The development of clearer standards was not before time. Some years ago one test publisher was seeking to define their own standards for access to a certain range of test materials. They set a qualification level as membership of the Division of Occupational Psychology (DOP) of the BPS or eligibility for such membership. They were taken to task by the then chairperson of the DOP for presuming to determine who the division might or might not admit to membership!

Test publishers have, in fact, been heavily involved in the BPS Steering Committee on Test Standards, and have clearly seen the need for appropriate understanding and competence in test use. Without such skills on the part of users the test itself – and hence its publisher or distributor – gets a bad name, and the value of its products and services can be adversely impacted.

The need for qualification controls has, of course, been evident for a long time (reference was made in Chapter 1 to the first courses in test use and administration run by the NIIP in the 1920s). Prior to the currently emerging arrangements the BPS operated a system of approval of courses in occupational testing. Completion of such a course typically led to eligibility to purchase and use a wide range of ability tests, interest inventories and careers guidance materials, but not personality questionnaires.

Eligibility with regard to the latter could be achieved in a number of different ways depending on the instrument concerned. Commonly it was through attendance at a specific course on a particular questionnaire run by the publisher or distributor concerned, but other factors would be taken into account, such as, latterly, being a chartered psychologist.

Level 'A'

Under the emergent arrangements the BPS is seeking to operate a two-tier certificated qualification system. The first tier, known as level 'A', is now in place, and qualifies people in the use of ability, aptitude and attainment instruments – the so-called tests of maximum rather than typical performance. Qualification at this level requires competencies in seven main areas as follows:

- defining assessment needs;
- basic principles of scaling and standardisation;
- reliability and validity;
- deciding when tests should be used;
- administering and scoring tests;
- making appropriate use of test results;
- maintaining security and confidentiality.

These 7 areas are sub-divided into no fewer than 97 elements of competence, all of which are required to be achieved for the overall level 'A' standard to be fulfilled. Those who have fulfilled the overall standard may be awarded the BPS Certificate of Competence in Occupational Testing Level (A).

One of the expressed aims of this scheme is to permit organisations considering the use of tests to assure themselves of the competence of those who might operate testing procedures on their behalf. To this end those certificated are placed on an on-line database register which can be used for such enquiries into the competence of individual test users.

The level 'A' scheme has only been in operation since 1991. It has been generally positively received and has gained considerable currency among those involved in occupational testing in the UK. Its development has necessitated various transitional arrangements. Under these those who were already trained occupational test users when the scheme was introduced were able to apply for a level 'A' Statement of Competence. Both Statement and Certificate are seen by the BPS as recognising equivalent levels of competence, with both permitting entry on the register.

How to achieve competence

The scheme was set up without specification of how or what training should be carried out to help people achieve the various elements of competence. Chartered psychologists who themselves held either the Statement or Certificate of Competence were able to sign an affirmation of competence for the test user concerned, which was regarded as adequate proof of competence for a certificate to be issued.

This procedure has now been strengthened by a process of verification. This involves checking the standards used by those signing affirmation statements. These checks are twofold. First is a follow-up of those affirmed to see that they are, in fact, competent. Second is the examination of the processes used in assessing competence. This refinement of the process involves a group of verifiers whose activities in checking on standards are, at the time of writing, just getting under way.

Regulation in test administration

For some time test administration as such was not systematically regulated. Although test manuals would make some recommendations, it was assumed that test interpreters, would learn test administration as part of their training. It was also tacitly recognised by many organisations that people other than test interpreters such as secretaries or other assistants, would actually conduct the tests.

As with any other professional procedures, though, there are key general requirements in administration and there may be traps for the unwary. For example the administration of certain ability tests such as verbal reasoning requires explanation of particular sample items. While the generally experienced and knowledgeable test interpreter may be able to do this on the fly, this would not be encouraged and could be quite challenging for a junior assistant. Difficulty, hesitation or confusion on the part of this person, as well as confusing the participant, may give him justifiable doubts as to the professionalism of the whole procedure.

This state of affairs is not, of course, helped by those organisations in which, sometimes after a good intention of specific professional training of administrators initially, further test administrators are trained by the first group of trainees – and so on down a slippery slope!

Fortunately, the carefully worked out standards for level 'A' as a whole includes the area of administering and scoring tests, as indicated above. This covers 12 separate elements, including arrangement of an appropriate quiet location for testing, use of standard instructions and dealing with candidate questions. Working to these standards and having understanding of them independently checked can give reassurance that this important aspect of the test use can safely be delegated, even though the BPS does not currently recognise a formal qualification in test administration as such.

Personality questionnaires – level 'B'

The second stage of the BPS scheme of qualification is the level 'B' certification process. This is intended to build upon level 'A', extending the scope of competence to cover personality assessment; the use of tests of typical performance. At present the precise details are still being worked out. A discussion paper has been circulated which, after due deliberations, is expected to lead to the level 'B' scheme being launched by the end of 1994.

As this part of the scheme has evolved it has become apparent that the diversity of instruments covered precludes a qualification as general as that at level 'A'. This has led to the idea of a qualification based on relevant general knowledge and core skills plus evidence of ability to realise these in relation to specific personality instruments.

Three broad aspects of competence have been identified, covering nine separate units of competence. The aspects are: *foundation* covering fundamental assessment issues in personality; *test use* to do with practical skills in administration, interpretation and feedback; *choice and evaluation* covering selection among personality instruments and their formal evaluation. It is currently proposed that unit weights be assigned to each of these. Accumulation of a sufficient and balanced set of weights will earn the right to level 'B' certification.

The current situation

The new BPS scheme is not obligatory upon test publishers. However, many of them have been intimately associated with it and appear to be giving it their support. The BPS themselves are actively encouraging them to limit test supply to those with the appropriate certificate or statement of competence.

Publishers may, of course, continue to set their own standards and may seek to do so particularly in the personality field. Nevertheless, given the level 'B' requirement for realisation of competence with identified instruments and given that the test publishers themselves tend to be the ones conducting training in such instruments there should not be too much conflict.

At present though there are some variations as can be seen by reference to test publishers' catalogues. For instance SHL lines up its own level 1 training course clearly with the Certificate of Competence (level 'A'). However, in acknowledging that some other providers' training may properly entitle people to undertake a shortened version of their course they indicate that prior possession of the level 'A' certificate does not automatically serve as evidence of appropriate training. The Oxford Psychologist Press refer both to level 'A' and to the forthcoming level 'B' certificate. In fact, they and several other test publishers refer to level 1 and level 2 tests. The domains of these equate to those covered by the level 'A' and level 'B' parts of the BPS scheme, but the existence of this multiple nomenclature can be confusing. Science Research Associates used their own system until recently designating levels 'A', 'B' and 'C'! Again a recent publication (Lee and Beard 1994) dealing extensively with the use of tests in the particular context of development centres (see

Chapter 7) describes the level 'A' part of the scheme without explicitly referring to it and uses the level 1, level 2 terminology.

Despite all this the way ahead in the UK seems to lie with the BPS scheme. Because the scheme focuses on behaviours required of the test user it also seems likely to give scope for appropriate refresher training and extension of skills courses to be developed. Such developments would go some way to minimise the decay of skills or 'driving test phenomenon', flagged in Chapter 1.

DATA PROTECTION AND FEEDBACK

The Act and the IPM code

The Data Protection Act 1984 refers to records held on electronic media. Many tests are now administered through computers and results automatically recorded. In other cases handscored tests may be entered into a computer subsequently for general ease of access or in relation to conducting validity studies. In either of these cases the subject of the test is entitled to know what is being held and to review the results. The number of occasions on which people demand such access is by no means clear.

The IPM Code of Practice on Test Standards (1993) refers to the importance of giving feedback on a test, without specifically requiring, under its terms, that this is done. Clearly this would cover the case of making results available for those tests held on computer file. The same code goes on to indicate that feedback should be given by appropriately qualified staff. Obviously feedback given otherwise, given the potential complexity of testing, is likely to be of limited value if not actually harmful to the participants.

Narrative reports: the role of the expert system

Further work may be required to extend the guidance given on feedback. The means of explaining test results in relation to computer generated data in particular does not appear at the moment to be well worked out. It is certainly possible to derive printouts with large amounts of statistical data which are often not particularly user-friendly.

A narrative report may well convey rather more. However, the production of such a report is not always feasible. They are time-consuming and require considerable expertise in their preparation. They may well be outside the scope even of many of those otherwise qualified and routinely involved in test interpretation. In addition, a report prepared for the guidance of recruiters is not necessarily in the most appropriate format for giving feedback. It will tend to raise issues of reservation or matters for further exploration as discussed in Chapter 4.

Alternatively, as mentioned in Chapter 2, a number of test publishers produce expert system reports with narrative plus accompanying charts and graphs which simplify the job of informing the participant about their performance on the test. The narrative part of an *SHL OPQ* expert system report is reproduced in Appendix 3. Such reports may represent the most feasible approach to feedback by the general test user.

EQUAL OPPORTUNITIES

Direct and indirect discrimination

The overall picture with regard to equal opportunities is complex, but briefly British legislation provides that individuals should not be discriminated against either directly or indirectly on the grounds of race or gender. *Direct discrimination* arises where membership of a particular category is used by an employer as a direct means of either admitting or debarring an individual. For example, to refuse to employ or promote a woman because she was a woman would be illegal on these grounds. *Indirect discrimination* arises when a procedure used to make or assist in an employment or promotion decision favours one group as opposed to another without the basis of favouring being related to the capability to do the job.

Direct and indirect discrimination are to be distinguished from positive action in which steps are taken to see that opportunities for an under-represented group are optimised, and which also requires the use of fair and objective processes. For example in the UK there is a campaign termed Opportunity 2000 aimed at increasing the quantity and quality of women's participation in the workforce. Many businesses have joined the campaign, as have the National Health Service (NHS). Their action points in the campaign (NHS 1992) include monitoring of selection procedures to take account of equal opportunities, helping guard against direct and indirect discrimination.

There is the possibility – not unknown in practice – of an unscrupulous employer actually practising direct discrimination and seeking to hide behind psychometric tests results to justify the following disproportionately low numbers of members of a minority group hired – described as *adverse impact*. Everyone will have some area of limitation and a wide enough battery of tests would point to at least one area of mismatch to a job in any one person. Thus, such an employer could find some weakness in test score to seek to justify discrimination. Fortunately such extreme abuses are rare and it appears to be much more likely that indirect discrimination will be associated with test use, and that that will tend to arise through error and lack of adequate consideration of all the issues involved. It is in fact in the field of indirect discrimination that psychometric tests have sometimes been implicated.

Litigation

Two recent cases in the UK involving indirect discrimination have been described by Kellett et al (1994). Both occurred in the transport industry – one concerned British Rail and the other London Underground. Both cases were actually settled out of court. In the British Rail case there were differences in average scores on tests between white and ethnic minority applicants for drivers' jobs. However, validity evidence indicating that such differences reflected actual differences in performance was lacking and there was, in fact, no satisfactory explanation for the differences found. Subsequent adjustments to the selection process have included variations in the trade-offs allowed between different test scores (see Chapter 4). By relating these to the standard errors of the scores rather than to score points alone it has been possible to find a rational basis for effecting a relative increase in the number of ethnic minority candidates passing the test battery.

In another case involving a test of English language ability an employer had claimed that the test would indicate whether or not applicants could read and comprehend factory safety regulations. The prosecution successfully held that the test used was one of high grade language capability which did not directly measure language skills at the relevant level. It therefore discriminated unfairly against those whose first language was not English and the employer concerned was fined. (If the employer had used a test procedure more directly related to the content of the safety regulations then the prosecution would have had a more difficult case to prove. Indeed, the likelihood is that the ethnic minority workers would have found themselves employed in numbers not dissimilar from their English mother tongue counterparts. Hence no discrimination would have arisen and there would have been no case to answer.)

One seminal American case was *Griggs v Duke Power Co* (1971). The use of general ability tests in selection was challenged on the ground that a relatively small number of black people were hired, that is that the tests had an adverse impact on this particular minority. The defendants' contention that they had not intended this discrimination was thrown out by the court. In the UK too it has been actual practice rather than intention that has been seen as critical.

The issue of validity

Most cases involving tests have usually turned on the question of content rather than predictive validity (see Chapter 1), as in the factory case cited above. Of course with many personality questionnaires, the content is manifestly and purposely somewhat obscure, but the test may successfully distinguish between higher and lower performers! Thus there may be some degree of conflict between the technical requirements of a test and its ability to stand up in a court of law.

As we have seen in Chapters 1 and 2 predictive validity is often a tricky proposition in any case. In relation to discrimination, one issue is that no one seems to be able to state just how predictive a particular test should be for it to be seen as a fair instrument. As we saw in Chapter 4 with a high enough cut-off even a test of relatively low predictive power may be of use to the employer. Applied with such a cut-off the test may well have some element of inappropriate discrimination against a minority group, that is allow them through in a smaller proportion than the majority group. It would also, though, clearly also be discriminating against many of those in a majority group who could actually do the job but who would not be in a position to bring litigation to bear in the same way as the minority! This idea is illustrated in Figure 6.1.

The complexity of such issues is reflected in the fact of cases continuing to arise even when there are apparently good intentions on the part of the employer involved. It seems that yet more exploration of the issues, more education and probably more probing of boundaries through case law will be required before employers cease to trip themselves up.

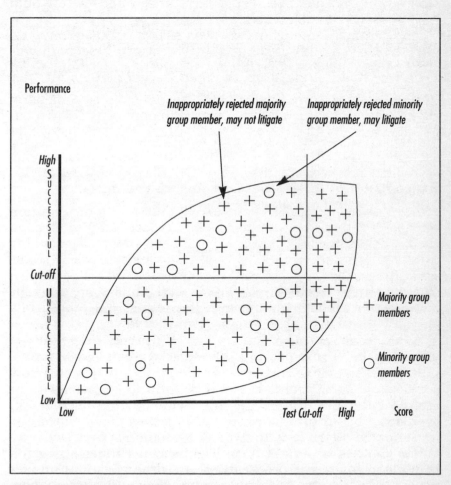

Figure 6.1 *Weak predictor and discrimination*

DISABILITIES

People with disabilities may also be discriminated against by injudicious or poorly thought out use of tests. In the UK any company employing more than 20 people is obliged to recruit registered disabled people if it has not already fulfilled its quota of 3 per cent registered disabled.

If tests are being used in recruitment, but their use is not adjusted to take account of disability, then they could become implicated in a failure to meet quota. The adjustments necessary would vary depending on the nature of the job. For example, in a job with a primarily intellectual content a disabled person with motor impairment could be inappropriately disadvantaged through the use of a speeded test of cognitive ability. Adjustments could include extending the time, widening the band of acceptable performance, scoring according to number correct out of those items completed or moving to a test with norms established on an untimed basis. Specialist professional guidance is likely to be needed to suit the particular case. A set of guidelines for testing people with disabilities has been published by SHL (Clark and Baron 1992) and should help those using tests in such circumstances to set their test applications along the right lines.

COPYRIGHT

As with other written materials copyright is vested in the originator of a test. Test publishers have been quite rigorous in pursuing breaches of copyright, committed either by users through practices such as photocopying test materials or through other firms passing off material as their own. It is still, though, not uncommon to find illegally photocopied materials in use (I came across a case in the same week as preparing the final draft of this chapter). Often it seems that this practice is based on ignorance. It may have been fuelled to some degree by the lack of controls exerted in the past.

The scope of copyright is, in fact, very wide, extending for example to charts and profile documents used in summarising test results. It applies, too, regardless of the medium used. In a recent out of court settlement Saville and Holdsworth Ltd gained agreement from another firm that the latter would remove an outline SHL profile chart from their software.

CODA ON REGULATION

At the end of the day regulation of various sorts is essentially for the protection of all involved. This includes those being tested, those using tests or commissioning their use or others such as test publishers, working in the testing field. Some companies concerned with their compliance with best professional standards will take the trouble to audit their test use, employing external professionals on some occasions or otherwise using their own internal staff. I came across the following situation when conducting one such audit.

A largely independent subsidiary of a major manufacturing group used ability tests to help select some of its operatives. The tests had been used for a number of years and the same test administrator had been employed for a long time, with the test administration forming a large part of his work. Over the years he had become blasé about his scoring procedures, claiming that he knew the right answers and no longer needed to use the stencil scoring key.

His management reacted to this in a novel but unenlightened way. They – by scissors, paste and photocopying – rearranged the order of the items in the test so that a number of early questions were placed later and vice versa. This also, of course, involved rearranging the scoring key which the administrator now *had* to use, being no longer able to rely on his memory in relation to the changed question order. The test was timed. It was originally designed with easier items coming first and moving progressively to more difficult ones. Thus changing the order of questions drastically changed the performance on the test and made the published norms completely inappropriate!

Regulation, of all sorts, although not yet necessarily perfect is clearly desirable.

SUMMARY

- Regulation of testing covers a range of issues from test design to competence in test use, the avoidance of discrimination and protection of copyright.

- Specific concerns have varied from time to time, as different regulatory issues have come to the fore. In the US and the UK these have been reflected in different emphases in regulatory guidelines.

- Standards in test design and use do not have the direct force of law, but poorly applied standards may involve the user in litigation.

- In the UK the BPS is progressively introducing a comprehensive scheme for qualification in test use, with clear standards for a range of practical issues.

- The Data Protection Act requires access by the subject to data held about him on computer file which would cover test results held in this way. Consideration of the most appropriate means of providing access is bound up with the wider issue of feedback of test results.

- Equal opportunities issues are particularly focused on indirect discrimination in which use of a test leads to an unjustified adverse impact on a particular group.

- Especial care is required when setting up psychometric procedures for those with disabilities, so that their actual capacities do not become masked.

7

Psychometric neighbours

INTRODUCTION

A number of procedures used to understand or predict behaviour of individuals and groups are generally regarded as lying outside psychometric testing proper. Nevertheless some of them involve similar or equally rigorous principles in their development or application. These neighbouring methods and their links with psychometrics as usually understood are the subjects of this chapter.

Like the mainstream of psychometric testing, most of the methods discussed here have been applied quite extensively. Particular patterns of use have grown up around each of them and they have their own strengths and limitations. Sometimes they may confer relatively unexpected benefits. For example, more than once I have found that the process of training line management assessors for assessment centre work has helped knit them into a cohesive team.

Broad and narrow band methods

Of the procedures discussed below *assessment centres* have a tradition and course of application that is well established in its own right having been used for many years.

Structured interviewing can, in its most highly developed and strictly applied form, represent a method as demanding and almost as precise as psychometric testing itself. Both assessment centres and some structured interviews focus on areas of competence and can be seen as narrowband. Other methods such as focus groups and some of the content analytic methods are more properly described as broadband.

Personal construct methods have sometimes been used to generate competencies upon which psychometric and other procedures are then based, so moving from a broad to a narrower focus. They can also be used directly to study individuals, but often in an exploratory, again broadband, way. This would apply in counselling for instance. In general broadband techniques allow one to identify what is important among a range of issues, while narrowband methods permit concentration on particular areas. This distinction may be helpful in considering the appropriateness of the different methods discussed here and their interplay with the more usually considered psychometric procedures discussed in the rest of this book.

A range of methods

In the study of body language, complex responses are examined in relation to complex patterns of stimuli. Psychophysiological methods sometimes result in tests, but the statistical basis of these is typically scant, compared with mainstream psychometrics.

Surveys and polls are based upon a series of questions, and to that extent resemble psychometric tests, but interest nearly always centres upon responses of populations or groups rather than individuals. However, attitude surveys and psychometric procedures can sometimes be helpfully combined. For example, a survey used to determine the required elements of behaviour to produce customer satisfaction in, say, a retail sales force, could be employed among other things to help define the psychometric procedures used for hiring decisions in future.

The formalised design and analysis of application forms using biodata methods can be seen as standing in a similar relationship to the traditional application form as structured interviewing stands to conventional biographically based interviews.

STRUCTURE IN INTERVIEWING

Conventional interviews – the research

The conventional or biographically based interview is probably still the most common means of making an assessment of another person. Despite numerous and repeated criticisms it continues to be used almost unfailingly in selection situations and has been discussed in this light in Chapter 3. In the survey of selection by Bevan and Fryatt (1988 already quoted in relation to other procedures), of 320 employing organisations, 263 or 82.2 per cent claimed to use interviews for all vacancies and only 2–0.6 per cent did not use them at all. For managerial and professional staff the figure was 90.5 per cent. This contrasted markedly with the use of personality tests with only 0.7 per cent of respondents indicating that these were invariably used in selection.

Among the critical commentators Herriot (1987) has described the conventional interview as no more than an episode of social exchange. Where research has been conducted it has indicated such interviews to be neither reliable nor valid in relation to performance on the job (see, for example, Heneman et al 1975). In fact in nearly all cases where the interview has been looked at objectively (eg Smith et al 1989) the conclusion has been that it is not really a valid method of selection.

Some attempts at applying structure

Over the years there have been a number of approaches aimed at bringing greater effectiveness to the interview by increasing degrees of systematisation. At the extreme, in what may be termed structured psychometric interviews the interview comprises preresearched set questions with set answer frames.

Along the way, though, there are various other models of structured approaches. The earliest of these was *Rodger's Seven-Point Plan* (NIIP 1952), which covered the following.

1. *Physical make-up*. Has he any defects of health or physique that may be of occupational importance? How agreeable are his appearance, his bearing and his speech?
2. *Attainments*. What type of education has he had? How well has he done educationally? What occupational training and experience has he had already? How well has he done occupationally?
3. *General intelligence*. How much general intelligence can he display? How much general intelligence does he ordinarily display?
4. *Special aptitudes*. Has he any marked mechanical aptitude? Manual dexterity? Facility in the use of words or figures? Talent for drawing or music?

5. *Interests*. To what extent are his interests intellectual? Practical – constructional? Physically active? Social? Artistic?
6. *Disposition*. How acceptable does he make himself to other people? Does he influence others?
7. *Circumstances*. What are his domestic circumstances? What do other members of the family do for a living? Are there any special openings available for him?

By setting out a number of areas that were required to be covered in an interview process, there was something of a common format. Thus the seven-point plan provided a means of generating data in a broadly comparable way, but without any clear pattern as to which particular sets of those data were likely to predict success in a particular job.

The emphasis on system, though, has been picked up in many other writings on interviewing, which in general stress the need for approaches that are orderly and likely to avoid the worst pitfalls that can arise. These types of recommendations do not themselves advance very close to the psychometric model. They are rather more geared towards removing other ineffective practices, for instance by helping to draw distinctions between information gathering and information giving phases of the interview process.

For example, Smart (1983) begins by pointing out the disastrous effects of wrong selection decisions. He goes on to implicate interviews, as commonly practised, in these. Based on his own experience of interviewing he estimates that only 94 out of 1000 interviewees respond honestly in conventional interview situations. He then produces a wide range of recommendations for improving what would otherwise be regarded as *ad hoc* interview practice. These range from ideas of building rapport with the candidate to the avoidance of leading questions. He also addresses the question of halo effects in which one or two responses from the candidate are used to build up an unwarranted overall impression, which may be negative or positive.

Other writers (eg Mackenzie-Davey 1989) indicate a wide range of good interview practices, such as how to get the candidate to talk. If the interviewer is doing most of the talking he is not only limiting the scope for the interviewee to respond but, again, as with leading questions will be likely to be cueing him towards right answers. The precepts set out in such books may well be supported further by training. For example, Latham et al (1975) showed how halo effects could be much reduced in this way. In the more structured interview techniques discussed below training is always a cornerstone.

Of course interviews are not just used in selection situations. Very open-ended questioning is quite widely used in counselling with the specific content of responses analysed. Similarly open-ended interviews can be used in explorations such as the development phases of an attitude survey or, indeed, in beginning to establish competencies. Such broadband uses are seen as effective and necessary in such applications. In selection, though, more focused, narrowband methods are much more likely to be helpful.

Criterion referenced and critical incident interviews

A considerable leap forward and a considerable move towards psychometric models came with the advent of criterion referenced interviews. Derived from assessment centre technology – which is discussed in some more detail below – the criterion referenced or criterion based interview requires a progression through sets of questions each related to a behavioural criterion. The questions themselves are not always tightly specified. There is, for instance, scope for some degree of follow-up, but the general pattern is more rigid than in the conventional or biographically based interview.

Because the emphasis is upon behavioural evidence, relatively little is left just to overall impression. As there is a clear framework for proceeding, the scope for asking leading questions or otherwise cueing the interviewee is very much reduced. An example of a set of questions in criterion referenced interview format is shown in Figure 7.1.

As can be seen a number of prompts and guides – if so/if necessary – are given and the interviewer is given some licence to explore further.

In practice several sets of such questions covering a number of competencies or criterion areas are used. The approach is demanding on interviewers more used to biographically based interviewing, hence the clear need for training. In fact the emphasis on behavioural data under the different competencies

PRACTICAL CREATIVITY

The ability to originate and realise effective solutions to everyday problems.

1. Tell me about a time when you used previous experience to solve a problem new to you.

2. Do you ever make things, perhaps in your spare time, out of all sorts of odds and ends? (If necessary) Tell me what you have done.

3. Tell me about a time when you got a new piece of equipment or a new system to work when other people were struggling with it.

4. Have you ever found an entirely new use for a hand or power tool? Do you often do that sort of thing? Tell me more.

5. Do people come to you to help solve problems? (If so) Tell me about a problem you have solved recently.

Figure 7.1 *Criterion referenced interview set*

compartmentalises the information gained and militates against halo effects, among other things.

It is not uncommon for those undergoing training in this approach, when the method is explained to object, 'but surely people can just make up the answers'. However such armchair objections quickly disappear when, as part of the training, they experience being interviewed under this regime. Then they invariably find that it is very difficult indeed to produce the behavioural evidence to support a persona that is not one's own.

Few studies are known of the effectiveness of criterion referenced interviews as such, possibly because they are rarely separated out from other procedures. Clearly a key step in helping ensure their effectiveness, as with any of the procedures under consideration, is to begin with the work necessary to establish the relevant competency areas.

Critical incident interviews

A related approach to criterion based methods is the critical incident interview, in which the focus is on a number of incidents or occasions where behaviour can be regarded as particularly indicative of subsequent performance. A mini scenario is set and then explored in considerable detail. In this way a picture is built up of characteristic behaviour. There may be an element of cueing in the scenario posed, but the pursuit of the issue concerned in some depth makes it difficult for the respondent to fabricate a response. Consider the example in Figure 7.2. A typical sales situation is posed and the interviewee is given an opportunity to respond. The follow-up questions explore the occasion in some detail. This contrasts with the wider range of questions with less detailed follow-up in the more common criterion referenced interview.

There are a number of other structured approaches to interviewing. Some of them, for example that developed by Rohrer Hibler and Replogel (RHR), use in-depth approaches conducted by psychologists. They will typically start with a detailed appreciation of the role in its context. Because of the degree of specialism involved, such methods are not readily transferable for management use.

Structured psychometric interviews

As the name implies and, as indicated above, it is with this type of interview that we approach most closely to psychometric testing as normally understood. Indeed at a quick glance the printed format for such an interview looks very close to that of many paper and pencil psychometric instruments. Questions are entirely predetermined, as with a psychometric test but unlike a conventional or criterion based interview. The interviewer may progress through as many as 100 question items. There is not the scope for branching and exploration that is provided for in the criterion based interview. However there

---

LISTENING

Sometimes a customer won't say directly what they want and you have to listen to the messages behind the words. Tell me about a time when you were able to do that to help the sale along.

- Why was the customer reluctant to say directly what he wanted?

- How did you check that you really did understand?

- How did you show that you felt it was OK for him to have the concerns shown in the hidden message?

- Did you actually close a deal that day?

- Is the customer still on your books?

- Had others had difficulty with that particular customer?

Figure 7.2 *Part of a critical incident interview for sales people*

may be some sub-questions that are asked on a conditional basis. For example:

> Do you ever get up really early in the morning to finish a piece of work? (*If affirmative*) Please give me a recent example.

The rigidity of format of this approach means that it is in general suitable for large scale applications and may be applied, for instance, in repeated recruitment even on a national basis.

Evidence and coding

Responses to structured psychometric interview questions are interpreted according to a coding frame. The use of this frame requires careful training. The end objective of this is to produce very close agreement among different coders, that is reliability. As discussed in Chapter 1, without reliability there can be no validity. While it is scarcely conceivable that the same degree of agreement among those coding such interviews could be found as would be produced by, say, two people using a stencil to mark an ability test, very high levels of agreement do need to be secured for the method to realise its potential.

Some of the questions put are comparable to those in criterion referenced interviewing, calling for examples of behaviour. However, when examples are requested the interpretation may hinge upon the number or specificity of cases cited. For example, in a question asking about creating good feeling in a team, two examples may be required for credit to be given. Typically such interviews are interpreted on a binary scale. Each response is coded as either evidence (+) or no evidence (0).

What constitutes evidence and so what goes into the coding frame is determined by research. In some cases the question may use a term or expression that is ambiguous or set out a statement so that it may be interpreted in a variety of different ways. Which particular way the respondent jumps will be indicated by the interpretative coding frame as showing evidence or not of the relevant competence. For example, in the question, 'What figures do you think about frequently?', the term figures can be interpreted as numbers or people, such as captains of industry. Only the former interpretation would receive credit. Yet other questions are open-ended, deriving ambiguity in that way, for example, 'How do you feel about ...'. Because of the importance of ambiguous items the interviewer does not interpret the questions for the candidate. In fact to do so would be to vitiate the design.

The ambiguous nature of some of the questions has much in common with the style of items in some personality questionnaire. Getting to grips with such aspects is likely to be particularly challenging to the trainee, but is clearly essential if the technique is to be used effectively.

Hybrid managers

The structured psychometric interview method was originally developed by Clifton and his associates in the US (see for example Clifton and Hall 1957), and has since been taken up by a number of organisations as users and/or developers. One particular development was by the consultancy company Oasis, working jointly with the British Computer Society to identify hybrid managers – those who could effectively span between information technology (IT) and the business that that technology was to support. In this case the research sought to distinguish between IT managers, general managers and what were seen as effective hybrids. Some of the responses loaded on one and some on two of these categories, but the overall instrument was effective in making distinctions among the three groups. Sample questions and format are shown in Figure 7.3. (For further discussion of hybrid management see Appendix 1.)

Telephone administration

Interviewing by telephone is perfectly feasible with any structured interview approach and is quite commonly practised with the structured psychometric interview. In fact the physical absence of the interviewee can be seen as underpinning the elimination of halo effects. Structure helps here anyway, but impressions derived from physical appearance are wholly eliminated.

OTHER CONTENT ANALYTIC METHODS

Thematic approaches

Any structured interview approach, with its need to analyse responses to questions, can be seen as related to other methods that look at the content of what has been said or written and seek to capture the themes expressed therein as a guide to understanding the individual or groups of people concerned. These content analytic approaches have their origins in psychometric testing and indeed sometimes use psychometric tests within their own systems, but essentially nowadays

OASiS/BCS

HYBRID HIGHLIGHTER

Page 3

No	Question	Mentioned in Response	H	IT	G
11	Have you ever managed to introduce a relatively simple solution to what others has seen as a complex problem?	Definite 'Yes', not just "I must have done at some time"	X	-	-
12	Outside work is there anything in which you have developed a special interest?	Mention of lack of time			
13	What experiences have you had that would aid you in making commercial decisions?		X	-	-
14	What does the term 'technostress' mean to you?	Does not name or has not experienced any	-	X	-
5	How do you decide waht advice to take and what to ignore?	Associated with technofear			
	How frequently in your working life have you had to adjust to new ideas or new ways of working?				
	Have you ever had experience of dealing with major changes?				

All rights reserved by OASIS Group plc. No part of this publication may be reproduced or transmitted in any form or by any means, electronic or mechanical, including photocopy, recording or any information storage and retrieval system, without permission in writing from OASIS Group plc.

Figure 7.3 *The Hybrid Highlighter - a structured psychometric interview*

Reproduced with kind permission of OASIS Group PLC

constitute a field in their own right. They rely on a detailed analysis of material ranging from relatively long and unstructured passages of conversation, to written information. Thus they are often broadband methods. They look at things like the use of intensives – very, quite, for example or the number of self-reference statements (I, mine, me).

These methods can be seen as arising out of projective techniques (see Chapter 2), but the material used is much wider. Their specific origin is in the work of Murray (1943) and the *Thematic Aperception Test* described in Chapter 2. The approach has subsequently been developed extensively with formalised scoring methods being applied to a range of interrogative approaches, though still largely based on motivational needs identified by Murray such as achievements, affiliation and power. A recent handbook edited by Smith (1992) gives considerable detail and is designed with practice interpretative material, so as to give guidance to the user of the method.

These techniques do, though, require highly skilled and studied interpretation and would not normally be seen as something to be recommended to managers for their own psychometric applications. One particular area for consideration of their use is discussed in Chapter 8 under mergers and takeovers.

Personal constructs – the repertory grid

Personal construct methods ask the individual about their typical way of looking at the world. Thus they provide a form of very individually focused assessment. They were developed by Kelly (1955) who produced an approach known as the repertory grid. A number of tasks may be used but a common one is a very simple card sorting operation.

The individual being studied is asked first of all to construct a list of elements. These will vary depending on the area of enquiry. Very often they will be other individual people. From a list of eight to ten such elements identified on separate cards, three at a time are drawn. The respondent is then asked to group the three into two that are alike in some way and one that is different from the first two. The process is repeated with progressive drawings from the set of element cards either until all combinations are exhausted or until no more types of comparison emerge. Within each comparison made the two ends of the dimension indicated by the groupings define a construct or idea used by the individual in classifying – in this case – people around him.

Once the initial sorting task has been undertaken there are a number of further possibilities. First, the constructs so obtained can be directly ranked for importance, giving another insight into the thinking of the person being studied. Second, the individual elements may be ranked according to effectiveness. Cross-checking this ranking with an importance ranking of the constructs and with the standing of the individuals on each of the latter will indicate how the respondent sees the different constructs themselves in relation to effectiveness. Although the method may appear laborious it can actually be undertaken quickly, often in the space of half an hour or less. It will frequently reveal patterns of thought to the respondents of which they themselves were not overtly conscious. Thus, it is likely to be more powerful than asking them simply to describe their perceptions of the world around them.

The method can be used to gain understanding of the person concerned in several ways. For instance, the number of constructs that arise in the process can be seen as evidence of the complexity or otherwise of their thinking. The particular constructs elicited will show how their thinking about the world is characterised. As such, and as mentioned in Chapter 5, it can be a powerful tool in coaching or counselling applications. In these settings a person's attitudes and beliefs can be explored in detail. The range shown in these ideas can be homed in on for further exploration. For example, a repertory grid may suggest that the person thinks about colleagues in terms of the degree of authority they seek to exercise over him. This could lead in discussion to confirmation of a desire for substantial independence and exploration, possibly using a mix of ability tests, of a variety of roles in which this desire might be achieved.

The approach can also be used to generate dimensions of competency or personality, or individual items for inclusion in further psychometric procedures. This involves making comparisons across the individual repertory grid outputs from a number of different people. In such cases, too, discussions are held to further explore the emergent ideas. Examples would be elicited as to the behaviour that distinguished the two people paired in the card sorting task from the person at the other pole. Similarly, asking questions about the implications of the constructs and why they were important for success would elicit the value systems of either individuals or a group. Also, asking how the construct would be identified in the organisation will yield examples of behaviour that could be correlated with superior performance and so be built into competency standards.

The range of application of the repertory grid method is wide. I have used it, for instance, in the study of roles as diverse as RAF fast jet pilots, female executives in the NHS and

management consultants. It is also capable of very sophisticated analyses and statistical treatment. A comprehensive and
clear basic exposition of the approach is given in Bannister and
Mair (1968).

ASSESSMENT CENTRES

Military origins

Assessment centres provide a means for a fairly direct
production of behaviour that is seen as evidence or otherwise
of a competency. They have a long history with origins in the
methods adopted by the British, German and American armed
forces during the Second World War for officer selection. The
original American work for the Office of Strategic Services
(OSS) is described by Mackinnon (1980). Combinations of
tactical planning exercises and outdoor leadership exercises
were used. The latter would include tasks such as building
bridges from ropes and pine poles, and transporting a team
and its equipment across. All this would be done to time, with
participants taking it in turn to lead or act as team members.
Officers would observe and rate performance according to
preset criteria. Such tasks were seen as fairly direct simulations
of what young officers, say those leading an infantry platoon,
would be required to do in practice.

Civilian applications

The method was taken up in the British civil service in the 1940s
for its fast track administrative class entrants. The first
commercial applications were in the US in the 1950s. Today
the method is widespread commercially and in government
departments. In the UK assessment centres are used by many
banks and building societies, major supermarkets, information
technology firms, food manufacturers and oil companies. (A
review of assessment centre work from the very early days on is
given by Bray (1985). For a recent exposition see Lee and Beard
(1994). For a long term follow-up study of civil service work see
Anstey (1977).)

Simulations and multiples

Assessment centres use exercises designed as simulations of situations likely to be encountered in a particular job or role. An individual's performance on the exercises, then, is regarded as providing evidence for the likelihood or otherwise of success in the role concerned. In the original developments success in the various outdoor leadership exercises was seen as evidence for the likelihood of success in the operational aspects of platoon command.

The approach may be applied in selection or in development. In the latter applications – termed development centres (referred to already in Chapter 5) – the results may be used to point the way for development towards success in a specific role or more generally.

Interpretation of the behaviour generated in the exercises is undertaken by trained assessors. Very often these are drawn from the ranks of line managers in the organisation concerned. They will typically pool the data gathered before their interpretations are finalised. They usually undertake this pooling under the chairmanship of a separate facilitator, for example a person from the personnel function or an external management consultant.

An important concept in assessment centre design is that of multiples: multiple competencies are assessed by multiple assessors observing multiple exercises. The exercises used cover some of the range of different situations or circumstances that may arise in the type of job in question. Usually feedback is given whether the centre is for selection or for development purposes. In the latter case it will be very detailed and form a critical step in development planning. As indicated in Chapter 5 the use of psychometric tests as such in concert with assessment centres is fairly common, either to supplement or complement information from the work simulation exercises.

A typical assessment centre programme, including psychometric testing as such, is shown in Figure 7.4. Figure 7.5 shows the relation between assessment centre activities and competencies, for the same programme. The most common types of assessment centre exercise are now reviewed.

Briefing 15 minutes   A - F

Numerical reasoning test 40 minutes   A - F

Interview simulation Performance improvement 15 minutes preparation 30 minutes roleplaying				Analysis Exercise 45 minutes	
A 1P	B 2Q	C 3R	D	E	F
D 1P	E 2Q	F 3R	A	B	C

Group discussion 45 minutes

A	B	C	D	E	F
3	1	2	3	1	2

In-basket brief and commence 30 minutes
A - F

Continue in-basket 45 minutes			Interview simulation - sales call 15 minutes preparation, 30 minutes roleplay		
A	B	C	D 2R	E 3P	F 1Q
D	E	F	A 2R	B 3P	C 1Q

Legend A - F = Candidates
1 - 3 = Assessors
P - R = Role Players

All complete in-basket 15 minutes

Figure 7.4 *Assessment centre for sales managers outline programme*

In-basket

An in-basket simulates correspondence relating to the role. Over the years these exercises have been found to be among the most valid of assessment centre exercises (see, for example, Meyer 1970). They give scope for exploration of a wide range of attitudes and ideas. Typically the respondent is required suddenly to take over a new role after the previous incumbent has died or become seriously ill. Other commitments mean that only a limited amount of time is available to deal with correspondence before they must leave, say to catch a plane.

EXERCISE

Competency	In-Basket	Interview Simulation Performance Improvement	Interview Simulation Sales Call	Analysis Exercise	Linked To	Group Discussion	Numerical Reasoning Test
Written Communications	**			**			
Financial Planning	**		*	**			
Operational Control	**	**		**			
Negotiation	*	**	**			**	
Service Orientation	**	*	**		*	*	
Staff Coaching	*	**					
Networking	**			**			
Perseverance	*	**	**			**	

* = Competency likely to be demonstrated.
** = Competency very likely to be demonstrated.

Figure 7.5 *Assessment centre competency coverage by exercises*

There are no other colleagues around in the office – it may be a Saturday morning – and the phonelines are not available.

The correspondence is seen as having built up over a period of a couple of weeks. It will usually be a mixture of issues competing for priority. Thus there may be time clashes between the visit of an important personage and the requirement to undertake budgetary planning. Sorting out these issues and dealing with other aspects of a short term nature may sometimes conflict with a need to get a grip on the whole organisation. For example, unresolved underlying tensions among the members of a management team are often indicated through a number of the items.

The content of such an in-basket has sometimes been described as rather like a soap opera. All the elements present do happen in real life in the job, but typically not in such compressed episodes! Sometimes the execution of the in-basket itself is supported by an in-basket interview, not unlike the skilled test interpreter's follow-up interview to personality tests (Chapter 4).

Group discussions

Group discussions vary between those dealing with general topics such as, say, equal retirement ages for men and women or the selection criteria for a particular post, and those in which roles are assigned. Where a role is assigned there is usually some degree of advocacy required, for example bidding for a share of a budget. Thus negotiating skills are often among the competencies examined in such an exercise. A limitation of the group discussion is that it is somewhat affected by size. In a very large group few individuals may have managed to contribute. Their lack of contribution means there is no behavioural evidence about them. This in itself of course tells us something, but may not tell as much as might have happened if they had operated in smaller groups. In a very small group the number of topics covered may be limited and individuals may form rather cosy alliances, limiting the scope for tough negotiation to emerge.

Interview simulation

These exercises are cast in a one-to-one format. Very often negotiation or some other form of representation of a supposed organisation is required. Other scenarios require the participant to undertake a disciplinary interview with a role player. The role player's function is to give the participant scope to generate the behaviour required. Thus, their job is to stay in role and to optimise opportunities for the participant to show his capabilities.

Such role playing requires specific training, as there is a need to give the participant the chance to demonstrate competency. For example a highly assertive role play in relation to a non-assertive participant would not only demonstrate the participant's lack of assertiveness, but could also limit his scope to show reasoning or planning. In the same exercise with the same participant, a highly accommodating role player might help bring out the latter two characteristics, but fail to bring out the lack of assertiveness.

Analysis exercises

These exercises are often based on case studies. The participant has some complex written and/or numerical material to deal with, and will be required to prepare a paper summarising understanding and making recommendations. They have some similarities with high level reasoning tests and, indeed, some of the elements within an analysis exercise will look remarkably like reasoning test items on occasion. Because the analysis is conducted as a whole exercise there is unlikely to be the reliability that stems from the item by item aspect of a reasoning test as such. On the other hand the scope to present a participant with a real life case – in which perhaps only the names have been changed – can be seen as a very powerful content valid aspect of the approach. Again, though, some degree of artificiality inevitably arises from the need to undertake such an exercise in the assessment centre with more limited time than might be the case in real life and, of course, without reference to external sources of support.

OTHER OBSERVATIONAL METHODS – LIE DETECTION TO BODY LANGUAGE

Psychophysiological methods

It has long been known that certain physiological states produce signs that may be apparent to others. Thus sweating, stammering and rapid speech may all be concomitants of fear. Increased pulse rate would be seen as a more generalised arousal response. Pupil dilation is associated with the observation of desirable objects and pupil contraction with the observation of things found to be unpleasant. To take these routine phenomena of bodily functioning into the psychometric field requires that they be made capable of measurement. To do this one needs to calibrate the extent of the physiological reaction to a given stimulus or input.

Perhaps the most well-known example is in connection with so-called *lie detection tests* using the *Galvanic Skin Response* or *GSR*. This makes use of the fact that sweating in the skin increases under a stress such as telling a lie. If a current is applied through the skin the increase in conductivity that occurs with the sweating will show in a detectable increase in current passed.

Other methods involve measuring changes in pulse rate or decreases in blood pressure or alterations in breathing patterns. These techniques are not easy to operate without laboratory facilities and the calibration is challenging. Although they have been used in selection such methods are not particularly accurate and, of course, are rather more focused on short-term states than the ongoing characteristics that are the normal domain of psychometrics. They can thus be seen as having links to another approach in the broad psychometric family, namely body language, which is briefly discussed below.

Body language

The formal study of body language is relatively recent with the seminal work in the field being that of Argyle (see, for example, his 1975 book). It uses the idea that body positions, movements and degree of physical rigidity give clues to mental states, and so can be used as behavioural predictors. As with the physiological measures such indications will often relate to temporary states or moods. However, there is also some scope to pick up the more enduring characteristics. Thus, when we describe someone as laid back we are using a figurative expression about mental attitude which we could actually see in a physical attitude or posture.

As with psychophysiological measures calibration is problematic, not least because of the ongoing difficulty of making determinations between transient and more enduring states. There may be more consistency in the interpretation of aspects of body language – that is in what it seems to mean – than in the actual behaviour to which the observation relates.

As with the projective testing techniques (see Chapter 2) interpretation beyond the merely superficial is likely to require considerable training and skill. At the most superficial level body language may be merely self-evident behaviour (the candidate who puts his feet on the interviewer's desk is probably giving a reliable indication of lack of fit to the company!). A danger is to use unreliable idiosyncratic body language cues, which can be as misleading as a pet question in a conventional interview. For example, those who are hard of hearing may sit closer and watch an interviewer more intently than others, and for one not aware of the disability this could be interpreted as showing great intensity of interest. Rigorously applied the study of body language may well add value to our understanding of a person. With its particular orientation to transient states though, it may be of more value in counselling than in recruitment or selection applications.

ATTITUDE AND OPINION MEASUREMENT

Surveys as psychometrics

The field of attitude and opinion surveying is arguably a psychometric area; another form of mental measurement. As indicated at the beginning of the chapter the focus, though, is not usually on the individual but on providing information about a range or group of people. Some consideration of this field is included here because, despite the different focus, the aim of such surveys is still to understand and predict behaviour on a systematic basis.

Statistical techniques are very well established in this field but regulation is perhaps rather less systematic than in psychometric testing as such. This is partly because the application of such surveys is much more diffuse even than that of psychometric testing. Market research, internal climate surveys and political polling all come within the overall span of efforts to use survey techniques to understand or predict behaviour.

Scaling methods

In fact the market research field probably represents the most sophisticated use of design and analytical methods. Advanced forms of scaling analysis are sometimes used to understand complex preferences. Methods have been devised to predict how choices between different products may vary with variations in their mix of attributes. For instance, at what price would a consumer not buy a car with certain safety features and how would choice be affected by the current brand image of the car manufacturer as a luxury, middle or low price producer? Statistical methods used to study preferences often involve probability modelling (eg Coombs 1964) to examine such preferences.

Other methods used involve a technique known as the *semantic differential*. Originally described in the 1950s (Osgood 1952), this requires the setting up of bipolar, that is two-ended scales. Examples might be strategy oriented versus tactics oriented, proactive versus reactive or lazy versus energetic. By getting people to indicate their views on a series of such scales their overall opinions are captured. Often ratings are made on the present and ideal state of affairs. Thus the method can be used in studying the individual as such and his view of the world. As such it has sometimes been seen as broadly equivalent to personality testing. More commonly it is applied to groups. The actual versus ideal ratings may be valuable in brand development or quality assurance work. The approach has also sometimes been used on a before and after basis, for example in evaluating the effectiveness of an education and training programme.

Questionnaire design and sampling

Complexity also shows itself in the political polling field where there is particular concentration on sampling techniques. The aim in both polling and market research is to make an accurate prediction from the responses of the few to the behaviour of the many. To do this attention needs to be given to the careful construction of questions and to choosing samples from which conclusions can be drawn. Questionnaire design has much in common with the methods used in psychometric test design, with debate on issues such as the form of response scale permitted.

Choice of samples upon which to base conclusions in surveys requires essentially that all those in the relevant population are equally likely to respond. In the political polling and market research fields this is pursued rigorously. In the former there is, of course, always a hue and cry when the pollsters get it wrong. In fields such as in-company surveys the same principles should apply, but in practice sampling is often less strict, with very high non-response rates often being tolerated. This situation is akin to that in the development of psychometric norms where, as indicated in Chapter 2, availability rather than perfect representativeness is often the criterion applied in finding people to be tested. Clearly in survey work as in psychometric testing proper the usefulness of results depends on the foundations upon which they are built.

Focus groups

Focus groups are a form of interview conducted with a number of people with some experiences in common. They are broad-band in their application. They are chaired by a moderator or facilitator, and are typically tape-recorded and transcribed. They have been used for some time in market research applications. They are also employed increasingly as part of competency studies. Thus a group of project managers may be gathered and steered through a discussion relating to effective project management. The interplay between them is important in eliciting a balance of views. The transcripts are studied to see what competency patterns emerge. They also yield case study items or scenarios that can then be used as part of the development of measurement procedures. Thus they might be utilised in producing a critical incident interview, an in-basket or a personality questionnaire. There are a number of books on this topic which may provide a useful introduction to the intending practitioner (see, for example, Morgan 1993 and Krueger 1988).

APPLICATION FORMS AND BIODATA SYSTEMS

The use of structure

The purpose of any application form is to gather information about a candidate, in the same way as an interview or a psychometric procedure does. Forms vary in the way in which they are structured. Many have little pretence at anything other than, in effect, reproducing the format of an interview that will follow them or capturing information comparable to that which might well have been supplied by a candidate in a CV!

Some people, such as Smart (1983) have set out systematic ways of analysing essentially conventional forms, looking critically at the information provided and producing ratings over a range of attributes. His particular approach is not strictly competency based – the range of attributes is much longer than a competency analysis would tend to produce. However, increasingly application forms reflect researched competency areas as such and seek evidence particularly relevant to the requirements of the job concerned. For example the Tyne and Wear Fire Brigade (see IRS 1994) use a form for firefighter applicants that asks them to give information about a range of relevant competencies including teamwork, physical fitness and manual dexterity.

Biodata – the actuarial approach

A rather different approach is the formal statistical weighting of different items of information. The method – biodata – essentially uses actuarial techniques. That is different life events are weighted depending on their impact on successful job outcomes, in the way that actuarial tables weigh different life events or circumstances in relation to mortality. This method is, in fact, the very antithesis of the competencies approach. It applies the weights on the basis of empirical findings as to what works without seeking to establish the causal linkage, which is the underpinning and essence of the competencies movement. As such biodata can sometimes throw up correlations with success that are not revealed by other approaches and this is its strength.

This relatively pure, unthinking, but potentially effective method was developed first of all in the life insurance industry. There and in some other applications numbers have been large enough to yield the necessary statistics to support the actuarial basis of prediction. Attempts are, though, sometimes made to utilise the same approach in applications far removed, where there is an insufficient amount of data to establish the appropriate weightings or even the appropriate areas to weight. The requirement for large numbers will perforce tend to militate against the method being able to deal with the need to represent minorities adequately in the research. Also, because of its historical basis of development, it may be inappropriate in settings where roles are changing fast. In any case periodic fresh research and updating is necessary for its predictive power to be maintained.

Expert inputs

Yet other methods lie somewhere between the competencies based application form approach and biodata in its purest form. Thus an employing company will make a determination of a number of factors that it regards as more or less desirable, typically establishing these on the basis of internal expert (or less than expert) opinion and applying it without conducting research in advance. Factors such as travel to work time or marital status would be examples.

Such methods may well have some validity if thoughtfully developed and applied. Without research, though, their effectiveness must be limited. (The strict biodata approach sometimes comes up with inexplicable links to success and, of course, these are unlikely to be introduced effectively in a non-researched – armchair – application). They must also be seen as leaving the operator of the approach liable to charges of indirect discrimination, for example if a particular geographical area is not favoured and is occupied by members of an ethnic minority.

Altogether, this wide variety of techniques relates to psychometrics at different points, threading in and out of psychometric testing proper in form and use. They may often have much to contribute, complementing or supplementing the mainstream of testing or, indeed, standing alone. How to approach the choice of methods will be among the issues considered in the next chapter.

SUMMARY

- A wide range of methods for understanding behaviour exists. From assessment centres and structured interviews to survey techniques, they may complement or substitute for psychometric testing as such.

- Structured interviews take a variety of forms, including criterion referenced, critical incident and what can be called structured psychometric interviews. It is the use of competency models and the systematic use of questions that distinguishes all of these from conventional interviewing.

- Other approaches, as well as structured interviews, look at the detailed content of responses to a range of stimuli or events. In the repertory grid the respondent generates the specific items to be studied.

- Assessment centres use a range of worklike simulations and trained assessors evaluate performance on these against competencies. The method is well established, going back to the 1940s, well researched and currently used by many commercial organisations.

- Psychophysiological methods and the study of body language are other approaches to predicting the behaviour of individuals. They are not very practicable for general use and may be more appropriate for assessing short term states than more enduring characteristics.

- Survey methods use underlying concepts of design and sampling that are akin to psychometrics. They are focused on group rather than individual behaviour.

- Application forms can be subject to rigorous examination and be approached on a similar basis to psychometric tests. The more sophisticated methods – biodata analyses – require large numbers to establish the basis of interpretation, and regular checking for predictive value against current needs and trends.

8

Implementing psychometrics

INTRODUCTION

So far in this book we have explored psychometric tests in general, looked at particular applications in selection and then in development, reviewed the various regulations and controls governing test use, and, in the last chapter, considered some procedures with varying degrees of relationship to what is normally understood by psychometrics. In this chapter we will examine a number of practical issues in the application of psychometrics, drawing upon some of the concepts and cases developed in the earlier chapters.

We begin by considering the accumulation of information in a psychometric application and then from this consider some of the logistical and practical issues involved. This is followed by a checklist of points to take into account in applying psychometric tests. In a final section of the chapter we consider some applications of psychometric testing lying somewhere outside the more common ones of selection, development and counselling.

INFORMATION FLOWS – BUILDING THE PICTURE

Capturing the competencies

As has been indicated throughout this book, no one procedure, psychometric test or otherwise will provide total information about an individual's chance of success in a job or the most appropriate path for development. Many organisations recognise this tacitly at least, but the response of some may be to engage in behaviour that is costly and dysfunctional. One high tech company, for instance, wanting to be sure that its sales managers were of the right calibre for the organisation insisted on candidates being interviewed by no fewer than 15 executives on some occasions. In that particular case psychometrics did not actually play any part at all. The company concerned had no systematic way of pooling the data and the poor candidates in effect experienced a similar process 15 times over.

Other organisations are, though, profligate with psychometric procedures themselves. It is not uncommon, but not particularly helpful, for an occupational psychologist working as a consultant to be provided with an array of results from different tests that may have been conducted at different stages of a candidate's recruitment process, or to be told that a referral to him was for a second opinion to back-up or presumably contradict what the company psychologist or personnel people had already concluded by some other set of procedures.

Nor is it uncommon for organisations to use performance, on the job or during fairly extensive training, as a selection process in itself. There may then be a recognition that, say, 50 per cent failure among trainees is regrettable but sometimes organisations will smugly say 'Thank goodness we did have such an exacting programme and that we did not have to leave it until the chap was actually working on the job to find out that he couldn't do it'. Obviously a little thought would have resulted in a more effective use of everybody's time, effort and money.

Information mapping

Consider the series of diagrams shown in Figure 8.1. This could represent any job, but for the moment let us imagine it is that of an area manager in a supermarket chain. Success in the job is partly to do with the competencies that the individual brings and partly due to the factors which may interact with these competencies. These could include management style – how supportive or otherwise is the regional manager to whom this post reports; trading conditions – are the other supermarkets cutting prices; or business processes used, such as the efficiency or otherwise of the company's just in time warehousing. An uninterested regional manager, cut-throat competition and a just in time system that turned out to be just too late more often than not, would all reduce our friend's success. The application of a psychometric procedure would be used with a view to determining some of what the candidate brought to the job that was of relevance. The test applied might be one of general intelligence designed for use with managerial level staff. An example would be the *AH5 Test*, comprising verbal, numerical and diagrammatic items.

The small circle, indicating the test overlapping with the large one indicating success, shows the effectiveness of such a process. In the area of overlap of the two circles the test procedure can be seen to be adding value. The part that is outside is, in effect, noise in the system as far as this application is concerned; that is, it distorts the message. How far the person using the selection procedure knows the degree of overlap will probably vary from case to case. It will depend on the general research done on the test and the specific work done in relation to the competencies for the job. It is evident, though, that the test will be more effective if it is chosen on the basis of relevant competencies, if it has itself been well constructed and if appropriate norm groups are chosen.

The same test may, of course, be applied more or less well. The use of inappropriate norm groups, rushed or hurried instruction and poor test conditions would all tend to reduce the degree of overlap between the test and what it was purporting to measure, indicating a movement apart of the two circles as in the second diagram in Figure 8.1. Our area manager candidate might be experiencing a selection process including a visit to a supermarket in the chain. The test might be conducted in the dimly lit assistant manager's office, which is not made too comfortable so as to encourage him to spend most of his time out front, which doubles as storeroom and in which the phone rings on and off throughout the test, despite protestations that it should be on divert. Alternatively, a largely inappropriate test might have been chosen, perhaps one just measuring spatial ability in the mistaken belief that merchandising layout would form a very large part of the area manager's job. Such a test might add some value, but less than the broader general intelligence measure.

If the supermarket had been able to develop its own *AH5* norms, then the precision of use of the tests might be enhanced increasing the overlap between test results and success as in the bottom right-hand diagram in Figure 8.1. In other cases it could be extra skilled interpretation of the test, for example by someone drawing on depth of knowledge to recognise a variety of patterns in a personality questionnaire, that would increase the area of overlap. The use of a follow-up interview specifically related, at least in part, to the output from the test results and probing the findings further may have positive or negative results on the area of overlap.

This has been discussed to some extent in Chapter 4. For example in recruiting a clerk the use of a cueing question as in 'You do not seem to be very conscientious – what do you say to that?' 'I deny it utterly, why only last week I stayed behind late every night to finish some filing' might lead to the interpretation that the test result was wrong. However a further follow-up, 'Why did you need to stay late, for filing?' as in 'Well actually it had been hanging about for months and months and I thought I might get into trouble if I didn't at last get around to it' might suggest that the original conclusion from the test was accurate. Though this passage may seem a caricature, it should serve to spell out how inept questioning can have an impact on what is gathered from the test results. Appropriate and skilful questioning can, on the other hand, enhance the information gained – in effect increasing the area of overlap of the two circles.

Combining tests

Figure 8.2 shows what may happen when a broadband personality measure is used, together with an ability test such as, say, numerical reasoning. The area of overlap with the competencies may actually be larger for the personality questionnaire. However, because much of the domain of that measure lies outside the required competency area, looking at the personality test as a whole could be misleading with so much of it functioning as noise. Returning again to the supermarket case, suppose the personality questionnaire used were the *Edwards Personal Preference Schedule* (*EPPS*) referred to in Chapter 2. Of its 15 scales several, including achievement, dominance and affiliation, might lie in the area of overlap. Other scales would lie in the noise area. These could include exhibition – a preference for being at the centre of attention – and heterosexuality.

It may even be that the increasing focus on big five

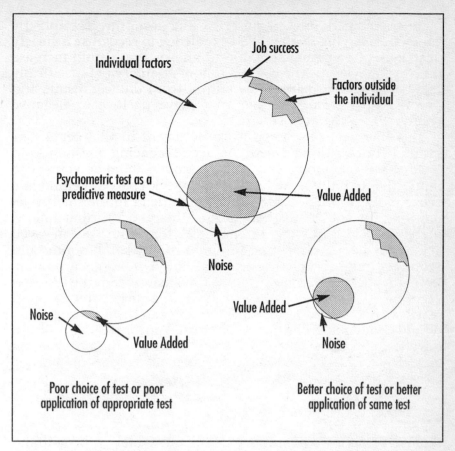

Figure 8.1 *Mapping psychometrics on to job success*

personality dimensions (see Chapter 2) would compound difficulties here. With such a broad sweep as the big five model gives there may be a compulsion to believe that somehow it is all to some degree relevant in all cases: 'Isn't it nice to have a general description of someone because you might come up with something interesting?' If the competency modelling has been thorough such a view misses the point. It may also lay the user open to charges of insufficient care in the use of tests. A finer grain personality read-out does not guarantee that consideration will be given to the question of what is relevant, but at least makes it possible and effective

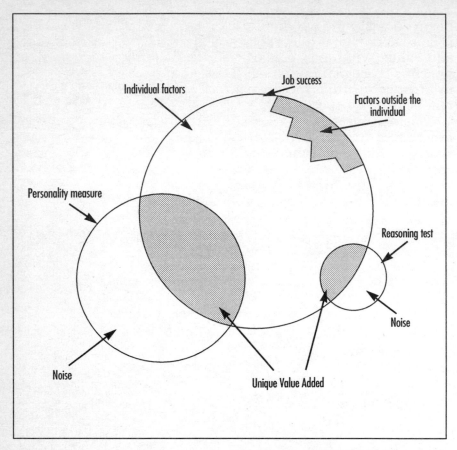

Figure 8.2 *Contributions of two dissimilar tests in predicting job success*

competency modelling would help determine which areas of the test should be given consideration in interpretation.

Note also that the two tests themselves are seen as not overlapping. Each then adds some unique value to the process. In the supermarket case the *EPPS* would not throw light on numerical reasoning ability and a numerical reasoning test would not tell us about motivation. Quite commonly, though, tests do overlap in what they measure as shown in Figure 8.3. In this case there is some unique value added by the second procedure. There is also some unique noise in each test which needs to be systematically discounted if the interpretations are not to be misleading. If there is no system for determining what is noise and what is relevant then all the data may be thought to add value. What may be particularly misleading, then, is that which is irrelevant but which has been measured by each test in turn, confirming the existence of something which has no real bearing on success!

Consider our supermarket case again. Suppose we had two test procedures, one measuring verbal, detail handling and spatial abilities, and the other numerical, detail handling and spatial abilities.

The area of overlap of the two smaller circles representing the tests within the competency domain is simply a redundant

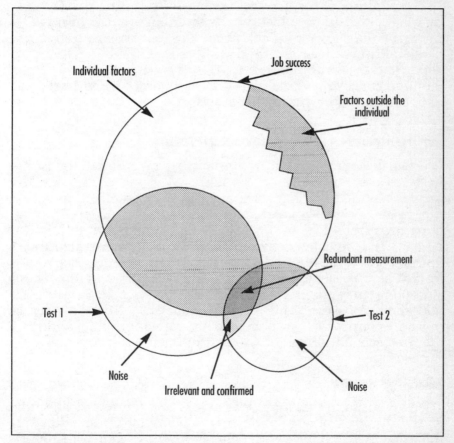

Figure 8.3 *Contributions of two similar tests in predicting job success*

measure, in this case the separate measures of detail handling. However it may not be recognised as such. Very often test users will take comfort in some degree of confirmation. Usually this is so because the precise area of overlap between what the test measures and what is required is not known perfectly, and it is also recognised that any measure is unreliable. However, there is a temptation to believe that because the two measures of detail handling yield a high score, not only is competence in this confirmed, but the candidate can be regarded as really having an extra high ability in this area. In this same case we might be tempted to take extra note of the two indications from the spatial scores, both of which would be largely irrelevant!

The addition of further and further tests or other procedures builds up the multiple picture shown in Figure 8.4. Ultimately, much of the domain of relevance has been measured – the personality characteristics and abilities that make for success in supermarket area management, say, but with much over-lapping, confusing irrelevant data and some of the irrelevant data confirmed by yet further measures!

Competencies and sub-competencies

It is worth noting that the systematic use of multiple measures in the assessment centre movement has, as part of its rationale, the very sound idea that competencies may, in effect, manifest themselves as sub-competencies, operating in different situations or different environments. Thus someone may be very persuasive in written communications as demonstrated in an in-basket exercise, but far less persuasive in meeting people face to face as represented in, say, an interview simulation. These situations may then be sufficiently distinct to require an additional measure. This is a different case from increasing measures simply because we are not sure about the validity of the first, second, third, fourth or fifth one.

Making sense

The way through this morass is at least moderately straightforward. Thinking about the domain of competencies, better still doing work to define competencies carefully and considering tests in terms of what they contribute is an important step on the way. Also note that, as a practical matter of time and cost,

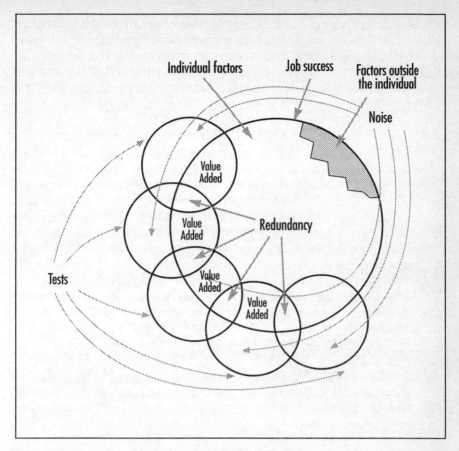

Figure 8.4 *The shotgun approach to testing*

relatively few test applications will be able to be undertaken with tests developed on a bespoke basis. Rather, in many situations, off the shelf tests will have to be used. This implies the particular need to consider actively what is relevant and what is not. As indicated already this may be particularly germane in the case of personality questionnaires. It is also important to consider the way in which the maximum value can be squeezed out of any one measure. Most benefit can be achieved with attention to appropriate test administration standards and meaningful follow-up questioning. In this last connection some interesting ideas have been developed by the test publishers ASE.

They have developed an interview prompt programme
generating questions to use in interview following application
of the *16PF*. The *16PF* pattern determines the areas to pursue
and advises on the type of follow-up questions. Part of such a
prompt set is given below.

SCREENTEST *16PF* Interview Prompts

DIANA ROD (Female)
Date of Birth: 10 Feb 1962
Date of Testing: 11 Feb 1994
General Information:
Comparison Group: Females:
British General Population

GENERAL STYLE OF RELATING TO PEOPLE

1. **Interest in People and Enjoyment of Group Activities**

   The responses suggest that a high level of enjoyment is
   derived from being with and working with others. Less
   satisfaction is likely to be gained from solitary pursuits or
   working alone. Questions might relate to feelings about these
   less preferred areas and the strategies used to deal with
   them. For example:

   - Under what conditions have you made a decision without
     consulting others?

   - How do you maintain your concentration?

2. **Openness**

   Diana has described herself through the questions as
   someone who prefers to be forthright and straightforward
   with others. The risk is that this may be seen by some as a
   lack of tact. Questioning might explore the extent to which
   Diana takes account of the impact of the way she expresses
   things. For example:

   - How important is it to be forthright in the way you express
     things at work?

   - In what situations do you control your natural desire to
     say what you think?

   - Plain speaking can often help to move projects along and
     cut through resistance. How has your preference for

speaking your mind helped you at work? In what situations have you found it less helpful?

- Your responses to the questionnaire suggest that you are forthright. What advantages and disadvantages have you experienced with this?

(SCREENTEST 16PF Interview Prompts copyright of the NFER-NELSON Publishing Company Limited 1993. All rights reserved. 16PF copyright of The Institute Personality and Ability Testing, Inc., 1956, 1973, 1982, 1986, 1993. International copyright in all countries under the Berne Union, Buenos Aires, Bilateral, and Universal Copyright Conventions. All property rights reserved by the Institute for Personality and Ability Testing, Inc., 1801 Woodfield Drive, Savoy, Illinois 61874, USA. All rights reserved. Reproduced by permission of the exclusive English-language publisher in the European Community ASE, a division of the NFER-NELSON Publishing Company limited, Darville House, 2 Oxford Road East, Windsor, Berkshire SL4 1DF.)

Similar guidance and prompt questions are given for a further 12 areas including several aspects of thinking style, consistency of performance and management of pressure.

Arbitrary criteria

The existence of good information from a psychometric test or tests and from follow-up questioning does not guarantee effective use of that information. Even when it is set out against a clearly developed competency model, with the intended contribution of each part clearly displayed there can be no complete assurance that it will be used effectively.

Anyone working in personnel or human resources must have experienced the candidate, excellent in all known competencies as evidenced by psychometric results of the highest order rejected out of hand by line managers because of, say, wearing suede shoes to an interview. Particular shoe-wearing behaviour has never, in my experience, been specified in a competency model or job definition and certainly no evidence exists of either positive or negative contribution to job performance. Nevertheless, the candidate gets no further. Painstaking thought about the psychometrics and attention to some of the practical issues outlined in the next but one section all militate against such arbitrariness, but there are no guarantees.

OTHER ASSESSMENT METHODS

Much of what has been said about building the picture could be applied to whatever methods of assessment were under consideration, whether psychometric instruments as such or, say, assessment centre exercises. So, how does one choose when an assessment centre or, say, a critical incident interview should actually be deployed? Inevitably this is like asking the proverbial question about the length of a piece of string. Certainly, with so very many psychometric tests in print there is reason to suppose that most competency domains can be covered. (I have put together test batteries off the shelf for roles as far apart as Spacelab scientists, factory managers and public school headmasters.) However relevant norms will inevitably be lacking in some of the more far-flung applications.

Some form of structured interview (as described in Chapter 7) may be thought a quick route to a highly focused assessment tool. However, to use the full power of that technology as represented in the structured psychometric interview is to embark on a substantial research and development exercise. Such interviews are, in fact, typically bespoke and so they do not offer the opportunity of ready off the shelf use. Their effective maintenance through training and retraining can be demanding. Their most powerful contribution to information is likely to be in relatively large scale applications where the scope for bespoke development can best be exploited.

Full assessment centres provide comprehensive information and would be unlikely to be appropriate at, say, the early stages of a recruitment campaign. Because they typically involve multiple participants as well as multiple assessors they are generally not suitable for counselling situations or one-off recruitment. However, individual exercises such as an in-basket may be very powerful information generators in such cases, not least because of the richness of potentially relevant and readily understood information that they may yield. Of the other procedures discussed in Chapter 7 some, such as focus groups, may be appropriate for use at the initial stages of setting up, say, a recruitment process. They would be likely to be of help among other things in specifying competencies. Repertory grid and the various content analytic methods, although flexible in their scope, do require specialised use.

FURTHER PRACTICAL ISSUES

Control and ownership of test results

As indicated in Chapter 6, when test results are held on computer file, then the subject of them is legally entitled to access. It is also important to give consideration as to who else may have access to them. Two criteria usually used are that they should be available only to those with a genuine interest and/or those appropriately trained in interpretation. One category does not, of course, necessarily imply the latter. In many organisations there will be people with appropriate training who have no real business need for knowing a particular set of test results. Conversely some individuals, eg recruiting managers, with an interest in results may not be skilled in their interpretation. Narrative reports, as discussed in Chapter 4, can be a significant aid if they are appropriately prepared.

There is also the question of where and how such test data should be held. Normally there is a need for some separation from other personnel files, which may be largely managed by personnel administrators, even for tests related to recruitment. Access to such reports also needs to be considered in connection with the requirements of the Data Protection Act and the need to give feedback, as discussed in Chapter 6. In the case of development there is likely to be an ongoing tension between the need to ensure the maximum level of confidentiality and the need to give access to test data on the part of those who may have a genuine interest in the development of their staff or, as discussed in Chapter 5, be functioning in the role of interested third parties. Abuses of access to test data are probably still sufficiently common to err on the side of caution rather than complete openness. You do not have to go very far to hear stories of people attending development centres where confidentiality is being stressed, only to learn that feedback has gone straight to a potential employing department on the supposedly confidential results!

Who should be trained?

Ownership of data and the questions of expertise that this raises leads inevitably to the question of training. We have covered this to some degree in relation to regulations in Chapter 6. The point to be made here, and which was touched on in the first chapter, is essentially how far to spread training and how far to rely on specialist staff either internally or externally. There are, of course, pros and cons in either direction.

The use of external consultants in relation to psychometric administration and interpretation confers the advantage of width and depth of experience, and a likely breadth of knowledge of, and access to, tests. They are also likely to have devoted facilities and trained administrators, and be organised to provide rapid turnround of results. However, consultancies may themselves develop pet practices with a limited range of psychometric instruments and have some inclination to utilise these, with some justification, but without their necessarily being the ones most apt for the particular purpose.

Of course individuals and consultant groups within an organisation may suffer from the same or even greater constraints. It does take time and money for training and also extensive use over time to enable even a specialist to master a new test process. The internal person may have limited time and be under pressure to fit in test administration, scoring, feedback to the candidate, and reporting the outcome with other duties and tasks.

The external person also has the advantage of a greater degree of independence, and may underline some of the points on confidentiality and other aspects of good practice. Indeed, he or she may be in a stronger position to walk away from or stand up to pressures from unscrupulous management in relation to inappropriate revelation of data or to requests to adjust reports to be more in keeping with some alternative view of the subject of the report. Such pressures are by no means unknown in the commercial world.

An issue that can arise in using an external or internal specialist in a psychometric application, is that the test or tests concerned may forever remain something of a black box. This will lead to limited comprehension by management of what the test can contribute. It can also lead to the possible disregarding of test results, in the way discussed in Chapter 4 and referred to

earlier in this chapter under arbitrary criteria. This is sometimes thought of as more likely to arise with an external
consultant – someone more remote from the organisation
concerned. However, such a person is in a strong position to
produce an authoritative report, indicating likely behaviour
and the significance of this in the role under consideration. The
external consultant will also be in a better position to make his
report and analysis truly comprehensive. For example, if he
should come across inadequate or conflicting test data he
would be expected to make use of further tests as necessary or
to complement the test findings with information from, say, a
criterion based interview. He is also more likely to have the
business and management knowledge necessary to interpret
the test results in a business context than, say, a junior
personnel officer, who might function as an internal specialist.

Another issue with regard to using internal consultants or,
indeed, of spreading expertise widely is that the practice of test
interpretation may become limited. This can happen in one of
two ways. In the first case the trained person simply has very
little scope for ongoing exposure to tests, perhaps applying a
single psychometric procedure only two or three times a year.
In the second case a single or narrow range of tests comes to be
utilised very frequently and, as raised above with the external
consultants, becomes a pet practice of the individual concerned.
There is no simple answer to these issues but they remain
matters for consideration.

Costs and benefits

I had an experience many years ago with a client who began by
stating that he wished to use a particular ability test. The
instrument concerned was virtually a museum piece and did
not appear to be the most appropriate for the application
concerned. Pursuing the matter further the real reason for
focusing on the test emerged – 'We've got a cupboard full of
them – management won't let me buy any more until they are
all used up'. The fact that they had not been used up quickly
because there were more modern tests available with more
appropriate norms was apparently beside the point.

Times do not necessarily change very fast. Recounting this
little story to another client, 15 years later, firm nods of
understanding were observed. However, closer enquiry re-

vealed that these were not signs of empathy but simply a signal that the same thing was being experienced by them. This client had a cupboard full of tests too: the consumables had to be consumed and the booklets used to dog-eared and scribbled-upon destruction before further purchases of any materials could be made. Relevance, competencies and standards were clearly not considered important.

Foolish as such situations may seem, they do underline the fact that tests are not free and users will expect a return on their investment before investing further. Thus it behoves those responsible for deciding upon a psychometric application to consider the benefit of a particular test purchase or particular training expenditure against its ability in the longer term. Precise costs of psychometrics will vary but in, say, a recruitment application are unlikely to be more than a couple of per cent of a salary. The benefits conferred are likely to dwarf such figures. If an objective psychometric procedure is not used, inappropriate appointments are much more likely. Not only is there considerable anguish on the part of the employer and employee, but ultimately the recruitment process with all its associated expenditure has to be repeated. In the interim damage may be done commercially to the business both directly and through the adverse effects on the morale of those working for or alongside someone who is inappropriate and may be manifestly failing. The cost of all this can be conservatively estimated as 200 to 300 per cent of salary.

Similarly, in development, the use of psychometrics will make it much more likely that an investment is well thought out, toning down the expensive knee-jerk 'Let's send him on a training course...'.

Physical considerations

Training in test administration will refer, among other things, to the control of the physical environment for testing. One or two other aspects are worthy of consideration. A company operating a large scale psychometric testing programme on behalf of a government department sought to update their test battery. The test development company whom they approached was a little surprised to find that one of their requirements was that the new battery should weigh less than the old one. All became clear though when it was realised that test administration took place at continually varying locations around the country and that the test administrators typically travelled by public transport.

Even today, some personal computers now often used for test administration would often better be described as luggable rather than portable. Also, where testing is to be conducted at a remote site it may be necessary to make the physical requirements known very explicitly. Space, light, quiet, desks, chairs and even electric power points cannot necessarily be assumed!

Briefing and practice materials

One of the trends in recent years has been the development of an increasing amount of pre-briefing material for psychometric testing. This is of various sorts. First there are books seeking to help individuals pass ability tests, by increasing their familiarity with material quite close to that which may be experienced in the tests themselves. This material is set alongside general guidance on the role and purpose of testing. An example is the 1991 book by Bryon and Modha. It is not clear whether the major contribution of such a volume is in the specific practice opportunity provided or in the general briefing on testing. Fairly clearly, direct practice of actual items is likely to lead to distortions of scores, but so could nervousness or lack of confidence stemming from lack of familiarity. Some employers' groups have opted to provide general briefing, seeking to demystify the testing process and give candidates the greatest opportunity of doing their best. For example, Banking Information Service have produced a booklet (1993) particularly aimed at helping young people understand the place of psychometric testing in employment.

A number of test publishers, too, produce specific briefing material on particular tests. These are designed to be sent out in advance, again to help familiarise those due to take the tests with the type of items that they will see and shape their expectations. An example is given in Figure 8.5. However, the use of such specific materials is very varied in practice. Their development appears to have arisen in response to requests from candidates. Further research and possibly firmer guidelines are needed to ensure a level playing field. It was only in 1971 that Vincent, writing about practical issues in testing from an NIIP perspective, warned against the menace of test sophistication, arising from deliberate coaching of candidates and the effects of test practice. Perhaps the wheel has come half a circle since then. The advice pro tem to test users is at least be consistent to your testees in the briefing materials with which you do or do not provide them.

The question of briefing also arises, in effect, in relation to repeated applications of the same test, which was raised in Chapter 5. The development cases considered there would often provide scope for control of instruments used within one organisation. However in recruitment one cannot legislate for what the candidate may or may not have experienced with other organisations. Some tests have parallel forms, that is alternative versions designed to cover the same ground. Parallel forms of ability or aptitude tests are more likely to offer a solution than those for personality instruments, where recent feedback may still be expected to have an impact on responses. In the personality field moving to a different test than the one experienced recently is likely to provide a better solution.

CHECKLIST FOR PSYCHOMETRIC APPLICATIONS

These are some of the issues to be considered in utilising tests.

■ What is the application?
  —Selection - internal?
                - external?
  —Development - current role?
                    - future role?
  —Counselling?
  —Auditing individual or team capability?
  —Team building?
  —Other?
■ Where in the chain of events should the application be made?
■ What is known about the role/roles concerned?
  —Competency model?
  —Job definition?
  —Established or emergent?
  —Does the intended timescale permit further investigation?

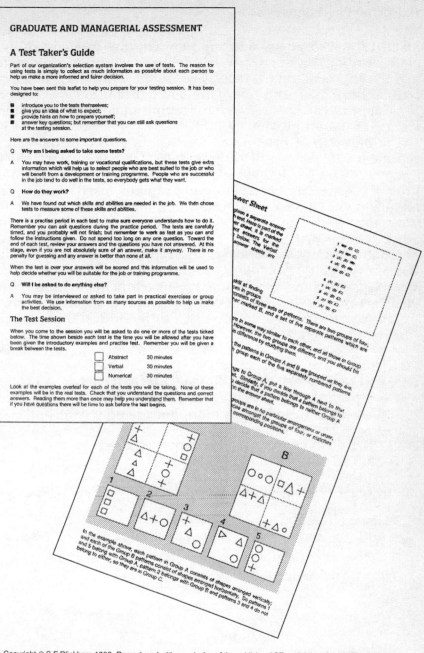

Copyright © S F Blinkhorn 1992. Reproduced with permission of the publisher ASE, a division of the NFER-NELSON Publishing Company Limited, Darville House, 2 Oxford Road East, Windsor, Berkshire SL4 1DF. All rights reserved.

Figure 8.5 *Test briefing material*

■ Have tests been used before in connection with this role?
—Which ones?
—When?
—Why?
—By whom?
—Are candidates likely to have experienced the tests envisaged already?
—What norms or other interpretative procedures were used?
—What norms are available?
—What were the results?
■ What resources are available?
—Money?
—Trained personnel?
—Existing test materials?
—Testing cubicles/rooms?
—Computers?
■ Who will have access to results?
—Personnel?
—Line management?
—Subjects of test – who will give feedback and in what form?
■ With what other data will results be associated?
—Appraisals?
—Outcome of succession planning discussions?
—Assessment centre outputs?
■ Will external or internal resources be used?
—Why?
—Who?
■ Is it feasible to undertake bespoke developments or establish local norms?
■ Will the Data Protection Act apply?
■ What other procedures will/should be used?
—Assessment centre exercises?
—Interviews – Structured/unstructured
                    – Criterion based
                    – Structured psychometric
                    – Panel
                    – Sequential?
—Biodata?
■ When and how will integration of these different data sets take place?
■ When, how and by whom will final decisions be made?

■ How will briefings and other communications be made?
■ Who is responsible?

SPECIAL APPLICATIONS

In this section we look at some further, special, applications of psychometric tests. We are still in the world of work, which has been the focus of this book, but away from the more familiar uses of tests in selection, development and counselling.

Takeovers, mergers and venture capital investments

It has for some time been a paradox, evident to psychometric practitioners if not to others, that in takeover and other investment situations the careful scrutiny of the books and other associated financial analyses is not matched by a study of the individuals involved. Thus, in deals involving many millions, tens of thousands may well be spent on examining the financial structure and potential markets of the target organisation. Some time will be spent in informal and, it must be said, relatively casual examination of the track records of individuals. This will be through conversations with the venture capitalists concerned, and through informal reviews using references and checking through a network of contacts. If one is lucky there may be an even less formal examination of their capability, as assessed by non-personnel people conducting conventional interviews. Rarely are the modest sums of money expended on psychometric testing that might help establish the book value of the management of the target organisation or help warn of the true character of a charismatic, flamboyant and resourceful entrepreneur standing on feet of clay!

Due diligence except...

The term due diligence is commonly applied to the systematic review of a target company's structures and finances. Perhaps in practice it should be better described as 'due diligence but with the psychometric assessment missing'. The reasons for resistance to the use of psychometrics are not hard to find. In some cases a variety of organisations may be seeking to woo the target organisation and anything that smacks of reticence is seen as a barrier. Of course, this fails to recognise that it is in fact in the best interest of all concerned if the best possible information is obtained in advance. It is probably due to the unfamiliarity of those commonly associated with such procedures that they tend to regard psychometrics as strange and unreliable practices, whereas junk bonds and mezzanine financing are seen as proper business tools.

Some organisations do apply psychometrics after the event, perhaps in putting together new management teams. It is not unknown for a new general manager, for instance, to use psychometrics in relation to sorting out how he will interact with his new range of subordinates. In general, though, the application of psychometrics in this field is both very valuable and very lacking. The particular concern that needs to be addressed here is clearly one of confidence of parties involved, rather than technically what particular test or tests to utilise.

This is, too, a field in which some of the broader range of psychometrics might very effectively be brought into play. For example, the thematic content analysis methods detailed in Smith (1992) and described in the last chapter could well be utilised. Although unsuitable for some other applications because of the very high degree of specialism involved, they may well add to the understanding of a target organisation in the type of work envisaged here. Of particular interest may be the work of Winter, described by him in Smith's (1992) book. He refers to the use of content analysis of a wide variety of verbal material, not requiring a specific assessment occasion on the part of the subject. A range of writings and even transcripts of television interviews come within scope of his methods, and one could envisage analysis of mission statements and chief executive officers' reports among other things.

Tests and stress

As has been reiterated several times throughout this book, tests are designed to give readings that are as stable as possible. Reliability is a key concept in psychometrics and wide random variations in performance are not a desirable characteristic of a psychometric test. However, this stability assumes set and controlled conditions. As mentioned already tests need to be conducted in a stable and uninterrupted environment. This suggests that, given a test that has been established as adequately reliable in such stable conditions, performance of groups of individuals on the test may be used to determine the effect of the environment as such.

For example, the argument would run that if a particularly noisy or otherwise physically stressful environment impairs performance on a test, then that environment may also have implications for performance on intellectual or other tasks required to be carried out there. There would be consequent implications for the initial levels of intellect required to perform such tasks under such conditions or for the amount of effort required to maintain performance.

Thus the use of tests to explore such situations can be helpful in determining how recruitment procedures may be modified and at what level the environmental stress is likely to become wholly dysfunctional. The research necessary to establish such factors is likely to lean more on the experimental than the individually based psychometric tradition and may well require the use of special, laboratory-based facilities. Such research is not particularly common but can be seen as a legitimate application of psychometric procedures and concepts (see, for example, Allnutt 1970).

More commonly tests are used in relation to making some assessment of an individual's temporary psychological state. Broadly based psychometric measures, including personality questionnaires and repertory grid, can give some indication of anxiety levels, which may have a transient element to them. Often follow-up counselling can be useful in understanding the source of the stress and giving guidance in a work-related situation.

SUMMARY

- Psychometric data should be regarded in terms of specific information required.

- Multiple tests should only be used in the light of understanding of their separate contributions. Otherwise redundant and/or irrelevant data may be gathered, wasting time and money, and potentially being misleading.

- If other systematised approaches are to be used alongside psychometrics, care also needs to be given to the specific or extra information that they will bring.

- The question of ownership of and access to test data extends to the matter of the association of such data with other forms of personnel record.

- Involving own-organisation staff as test users will confer benefits of ownership, but will not usually bring the level of expertise and focused commitment that an external consultancy can bring.

- Costs of using psychometrics are slight in proportion to the benefits that they can confer.

- Briefing and practice materials may help test participants feel more comfortable about the procedures they are undertaking, and so enhance the accuracy of test findings.

- Psychometric procedures are not widely applied in connection with mergers and takeovers, management buy-ins or venture capitalist investments, but potentially have much to offer in such cases.

- Tests are sometimes used to assess a short term state of stress in an individual. Sometimes they are used to assess effects, such as those arising from adverse environments, on groups of people.

9

Conclusions

A BALANCE SHEET – OR NOT?

At this stage of a book on such a practically oriented subject as psychometrics it is tempting to seek to draw up a balance sheet listing pros and cons. The temptation will be resisted, for as with many other procedures there is really no perfect answer to the question of the contribution of psychometrics. Used with care and thought they can undoubtedly add value, exploring parts not reached by other mechanisms, and doing so in a much more systematic and objective way. Applied in slapdash fashion without consideration for context of use, the information base on which the particular application is founded or the skills of those charged with their wider interpretation they can be meaningless or positively harmful. It is thus only through careful and systematic application that the benefits of psychometrics that were set out at the beginning of Chapter 1 will actually be realised.

Rather than drawing up a strict list of points favourable and unfavourable to psychometrics we will instead in this chapter first make some observations on the perceived role of the test user and then go on to consider a number of particular areas surrounding the use of tests.

PSYCHOMETRICS AND MYSTERY

The desire for the mystical

One of the more curious aspects of the application of tests is that one comes up time and again against what one may describe as a desire for the mystical. It is in this that there seems to reside some of the failure of psychometrics to attain the routine and systematic application of other systems used in business and elsewhere – a point made in the first chapter. It also leads to a great deal of ambivalence about the value and position of testing. It is by no means uncommon to find oneself in the midst of a serious discussion about a candidate based on comprehensive and exhaustive study using a well-prepared psychometric battery, only to find the conversation interrupted by an enquiry as to the candidate's birth sign. Although this is as often as not followed by a rather shame-faced 'but I don't suppose you believe in any of that', the occurrence of such comments is sufficiently frequent to make a practitioner of psychometrics believe that such thoughts about the mystical influences upon people are deep-rooted.

This desire for pursuit of the mystical seems to show itself in other ways as well. Anyone who has worked with a competency system and, in particular, has used such a system within a definition as broad as that of Evarts (1987) – 'Underlying characteristic of the manager causally related to superior performance on the job' – cannot but be struck by the frequent desire for there to be other things outside the competency domain yet somehow relevant to the issues in question. 'I wouldn't really call that a competency, but surely there's a question of fit, what about chemistry?' are typical and frequent comments.

Of course, as with most other issues of complexity there is at least a grain of truth here. There may be transient situations operating upon the individual, for example a fear of redundancy, affecting their capability or willingness to deploy the competencies that they have. Even such states could, though, be at least partly inferred from or interpreted in relation to the motivational element of the competency pattern found. Altogether this sort of reservation reflects comments that many of those using psychometrics or advocating their use will have heard over the years. Total rejection of the idea of systematic measurement is contained in statements such as 'I don't want anyone with a beard', 'I can tell whether I like someone by the firmness of their handshake'; or 'I can tell in the first ten seconds whether this person will fit in'. These are not just rare and amusing quotations but comments made probably every day of the week by serious minded executives and business people. But why should it be so?

Experts on people

People are certainly complex and yet we are all somehow or another experts on people. If someone carrying a test manual comes along – thereby signifying a claim to greater or special expertise – then the special personal, intuitive understanding of others that is so widely claimed, albeit tacitly, is challenged. The idea that everyone thinks they are a good interviewer was raised in Chapter 3 and is one manifestation of this self-assumed expertise. Casual and quick methods from the handshake appraisal on are not demanding to cope with and use either.

The fact that tests do not work perfectly and that experts sometimes disagree among themselves on such absolutely fundamental issues as what is personality and what is intelligence – which issues have actually been circumvented in this book – does not, of course, help the way to clearer understanding! It is, perhaps, worth noting that some journalists – ever with an instinct for the fundamental impulses that drive people on – so frequently write negatively about psychometrics. What is also interesting is that all the articles are virtually identical. Two or three cases are cited – individual cases not studies – some favouring and some contrary to the value of psychometrics – the evil spirit must not be altogether dispatched in the first paragraph. A couple of experts are quoted with views that do not entirely agree, even if they are not wholly opposed. As the final blow a couple of test items are quoted – necessarily entirely out of context – but implicitly or explicitly criticising face validity – to prove how nonsensical the whole process is.

Magic and Rasputin

Parry, a pioneering figure in British psychology writing in 1951 addressed similar issues. He said:

> in the minds of the public the psychologist is the man who has sought to destroy magic by showing that the need for it originates in the mind ... the need, however, being indestructible, the public performs the subtle operation of transferring magical powers to the supposed destroyer. Hence the psychologist becomes a witch doctor, a dealer in black magic, a sinister object whose menace is most easily neutralised by ridicule.

It is the desire for magic that, perhaps, more than anything else, keeps graphology alive and the service of neutralising by ridicule that some journalists so readily seem to apply to psychometrics. It is, perhaps, too, the recognition of the value of the witch doctor figure – the back pocket Rasputin – that has inclined some executives in the past to seek to align themselves with psychometric psychologists available when required to be called in as a second opinion, but not being allowed to position themselves so that their services can ever be entered into the mainstream of considerations about people. All this is to say, in effect, that the intending user of psychometrics, more often than not a non-psychologist these days, should be prepared to cope with the irrational as well as the rational.

GLOBALISATION?

The transferability of Western English speaking/ approaches

This book has concentrated particularly on the use and application of psychometrics within the UK context, albeit with substantial reference to developments and practice in the US. More and more organisations operate, of course, on a global basis and so the question arises as to how far in using tests one may be able to operate internationally. The answer is, of course, 'It all depends'.

Where there are some commonalities of culture as, say, among Western European nations, then the practice of translating tests into different languages would seem to be a starting point. However there are complications. For instance in France there have been different traditions from the UK, with much greater emphasis on projective techniques and upon graphology. One fairly recent study (Shackleton and Newell 1991) looked in detail at methods used in selection in that country, compared to the UK. In their survey sample 77 per cent of the French firms used graphology, while only 2.6 per cent of British firms did. In Britain there was a higher use of cognitive reasoning tests: 69.9 per cent compared with 48.9 per cent in France.

A number of writers, such as Cherns (1982) and Hofstede (1984) have described systematic cultural differences in

Europe. These would go some way to account for such differences in psychometric practice between two nations. Of course they also complicate the picture as far as seeking to work on a basis of common understanding goes, particularly in terms of personality measurement.

Rejection or balance?

Moving further afield, some writers have gone so far as to reject Western English speaking traditions entirely in psychometrics. Thus Akin-Ogundeji (1991), writing from experience in Nigeria, has tended to reject the entirety of Western-oriented psychological practices for Africa. Others, such as Carr and MacLachlan (1993) have advocated less extreme approaches in which imported psychometrics are to be critically reviewed so that the most relevant can be utilised, but in which the development of local procedures is also to be encouraged. Among the different cultural aspects to which they refer, in considering the particular case of Malawi, are the local perceptions of the meaning of work itself. Clearly any occupationally oriented process that does not take due note of such fundamental concepts is unlikely to be of much use.

The implications are not only for how particular tests, especially personality questionnaires, might be interpreted by those taking them in these countries, but also for the competencies themselves that would make for success in different settings. It does seem to make more sense, in many circumstances, not to seek to over-globalise but to aim to use local expertise and local development.

These considerations also indicate the value of considering locally applied assessment centres and structured interview techniques, with their scope to focus directly on behaviour.

Local adaptations

In putting together a major recruitment activity for an American organisation operating in Europe some years ago my colleagues and I found ourselves faced with a clear and effective description of competencies, based upon research, a strong requirement to undertake psychometric testing but, at that time, no common methods among the participating countries. What soon became evident, though, was that the range of tests available in each of those countries was sufficiently wide to provide effective screening devices. Ultimately, after much deliberation among the consultants concerned they all felt they had produced a fair basis for comparison. Nevertheless this was to some degree the application of judgement rather than pure science!

Producing local norms is generally recommended when using ability tests outside their country of origin. Even the most abstract of such tests will not be entirely culture free. Irvine et al (1990) point out, for instance, that any ability test presupposes some specific knowledge before it can be applied meaningfully.

Some studies have sought to show just where and how far particular instruments may be used. For example, Evans and Sculli (1981) described the application of a US personality inventory in Hong Kong. The particular inventory used was one that appeared to identify characteristics associated with effective management in its country of origin. They found very similar patterns of results but with overall differences, which they attributed to differences in the level of cultural development in the two countries. Differences in response to particular items in the same study were in line with the oriental concept of face. Labels that would be associated with loss of face, such as immature or irritable, were not endorsed in Hong Kong. Thus, some parts of the model captured in the inventory appeared relevant in the culture to which it was displaced, but there was also an evident need for considerable care in interpretation.

Altogether in this area for the future we can see that a great deal of further work is needed. Western English speaking models will not always be appropriate, but their wholesale rejection for use outside their cultures of origin would be to deny much that could be of value.

META-ANALYSIS

In Chapters 1 and 2 we referred to some of the difficulties in establishing validity adequately. Some of these difficulties reflected the very small numbers of people sometimes available as research subjects. One approach that has offered a partial way out of these difficulties is that of meta-analysis, in which a variety of different studies may be combined together and an overall result produced. The techniques involved are relatively new (see, for example, Schmidt and Hunter 1977). They depend upon the pooling of data from different studies in order to demonstrate validity.

Sample size

The reason why small samples do not work for purposes of validation is that the chance of misleading results occurring by accident is heightened when the number of observations is small, as illustrated below.

> Consider the following situation. A bag contains nine red balls and one white ball. A ball is picked at random. The chances of it being white are one in ten or 10 per cent. If an inference is made on the basis of this single sample then the wrong inference would be made on 10 per cent of occasions on which such an experiment was undertaken. Supposing, however, that the first ball is replaced and the second one drawn before any conclusion is made. The chance of two successive drawings being white, and so giving the wrong impression, is 1 per cent. Thus, as the sample size increases the chances for a misleading picture to arise diminishes. It is this simple fact of sampling that is the basis of most currently applied statistical methods.

Statistical tests applied to research results from psychometrics and elsewhere are typically based on what is called null hypothesis testing. The null hypothesis is the hypothesis that there is no difference between two populations, as evidenced by the sample drawn. The convention is that the chance of the observed findings having arisen needs to be less than 1 in 20 before the null hypothesis can be rejected and a true difference can be said to exist. With small samples the chance variations are just too large for the necessary difference to be established. Meta-analysis can be seen as, in effect, a way of increasing sample size and thereby getting over this difficulty.

It is also worth noting that there are likely to be further statistical developments, as well as further developments in other aspects of psychometrics. This is exemplified by very recent work by Bartram (1994) on the way in which the well-established statistic, the standard error (see Chapter 4), may be interpreted. Thus, part of the continued development of psychometrics is likely to involve the continued development of the supporting research and statistics.

THE USE OF COMPUTERS IN PSYCHOMETRICS

Number crunching to norms

The early use of computers in connection with psychometric testing was to do with the analysis of research data. Previously laborious hand calculation methods had been employed to work through the extensive correlations necessary to support large correlational studies. It might take a researcher up to a year to complete a complex analysis of data (such as a factor analysis) from a single study by hand. Subsequently computers came to be used increasingly for the administration and scoring of tests. This is an area which appears to have some further way to go as yet.

A note of caution certainly should be sounded in relation to the norming of test procedures. Norms developed on a paper and pencil basis of administration may not necessarily apply, particularly to an ability test with time constraints, when administered by a computer. Variations in behaviour with computer administrations appear to include the extent of the tendency to scan forward and back to review answers. With some applications in which a test booklet is still used in conjunction with the computer administration, there may be variations in visual scanning patterns of the material, which can affect speed of response. In the most professional applications standardisation will have been undertaken with the computer administration so that appropriate normative comparisons can be made. It is also evident, though, that the skill of software specialists in putting a test on to a computer may often outstrip their expertise in the area of testing as such and it would appear that there may well be some enthusiastic computerisations where the necessary background work has not in fact been done!

Some of the difficulties of translating from one medium to another, in this case from paper and pencil to film, were reviewed in a study by Ridgway (1977). He concluded that in effect a different test had been produced with the change to the new medium. Another matter for caution is when using tests in mixed mode; eg with some computer and some paper and pencil administration. This can sometimes be the case where a sudden increase in the numbers of people required to be tested outstrips the supply of computer terminals available.

Selection and generation of items

Another development that has taken place is the use of computers in item selection. As mentioned in Chapter 2 in some cases items are generated in relation to an adaptive model, so that difficulty is adjusted depending on the performance of the person undertaking the tests. It is not clear why this movement which seemed to hold promise some years ago does not seem to have been taken very much further in recent years. A more recent development is, though, the use of computers not only to deliver and select items but actually to generate them. Among other things this solves the problem of repeated exposure to the same tests. The work of Irvine et al (1990) is in this direction and seems to give scope for further effective exploitation.

FINAL COMMENTS

We have already referred in this chapter to work that may be required in the future. Further increases in integrated approaches, linking testing with other human resource activities have been anticipated in publications such as those by Toplis et al (1987). For such integration to be effective there does need to be an increased recognition of what psychometric tests are. They are essentially management tools which can help bring some order to the intriguing task of understanding and predicting those most complex of phenomena, human behaviour. Despite popular protestations to the contrary, their tradition is scientific, not magical, and their design and use are governed by system, order and rational thought, and the collection of data, not by whim or wizardry.

There is still much to be done if psychometrics are truly to deliver their full potential. Cronbach (1966) claimed 'Interpretations of test data are daily creating better lives by guiding a man into a suitable lifework ...'. Current psychometric writers are perhaps more critical of their craft. Robertson (1994), for instance, claims a need for more research into something as fundamental as the role of general mental ability in work performance. (And, as indicated earlier in this chapter, there is certainly some way to go in terms of cross-cultural work.)

The need for broadening of thinking and linking into a wider conceptual framework has also been echoed by Fletcher (1994) in a review of priorities and principles in test use. It is to such a broadening that I hope this volume will have contributed.

Appendix 1

Comments and technical notes

NORMAL CURVE

The normal curve is sometimes referred to as the Gaussian distribution after the nineteenth-century mathematician Gauss, although it was actually discovered in the eighteenth century by De Moivre. As it is strictly a continuous distribution the representation of the y-axis or ordinate as 'number of cases' is inappropriate. Numbers of cases lying between two points on the x-axis or altogether below a single point on that axis would be found by mathematical integration of the function describing the normal curve between the two points or below the single point respectively. However, the 'number of cases' labelling of the y-axis is common in general discussions and appears usefully illustrative.

CORRELATION COEFFICIENT

The correlation coefficient is a fundamental statistic in psychometrics. It is the way in which predictive, content and concurrent validity are expressed. Reliability is also indicated by a correlation coefficient, but termed then the reliability coefficient. It may be determined in that case in several different ways, the most common by using repetitions of the same test or by making comparisons of performance on two halves of the same test – the split half method.

Correlation is also the cornerstone of factor analytic and other multivariate methods.

Very often in conducting validity studies the measure of

success will be less detailed than the test score. It may only be possible to regard people as falling into a rank order of performance, or divided into effective or ineffective performers. Fortunately different forms of correlation coefficient are available to cover such cases.

MULTIPLE REGRESSION

In calculating a multiple regression equation one needs to know the separate correlations of each test with performance on the behavioural variable of interest and the correlations among each of the tests. If the correlations between two tests were particularly high then the second of them to be considered would add little to the ability to predict behaviour given by the first of them.

Multiple regression equations are of the form: Performance = W1 T1 + W2 T2 + W3 T3 + ... WN TN + C, where W1 – WN are the weights to be applied to standardised test scores T1 – TN and C is a constant.

For example, suppose sales performance was predicted from a battery of three tests for which we had sten scores, the multiple regression equation might be as follows: Sales (£,000) = 3.3(4) + 2.8(5) + 6(8) + 5. Here the third test indicated has the highest correlation with sales, as reflected in the higher weight for that test (6).

FACTOR ANALYSIS

Factor analysis is the name given to one set of multivariate techniques, that is methods for studying the interplay among groups of variables. By looking at patterns of correlation among test items they show how the items group together to form factors. To the extent that these factors are comprehensible they may be used as descriptors of abilities or of dimensions of personality.

Other multivariate methods are used in market research to see, for example, how different groups of consumers may be clustered together.

Factor analysis is used to reduce the number of dimensions in a range of tests by examining the correlations among the test scores. Groups of tests with high correlations would be described as reflecting a general factor, while those with low intercorrelations would represent a specific factor. Although starting with the fairly simple idea of correlation, the statistical methods used are complex and varied. The wider field of multivariate analysis of which factor analysis is a part also includes regression analysis.

HYBRID MANAGERS

The concept of hybrid management is of fairly recent coinage, being first used by Earl (1989). He described them as people with strong technical skills and adequate business knowledge or vice versa. The technical skills referred to are usually understood to be those of information technology (IT). Their significance in harnessing the power of IT has been discussed by a number of writers, eg Palmer (1990), Edenborough (1990). A number of British universities and business schools have set up masters' programmes in hybrid management. For example, since 1992 Sheffield Hallam University has been delivering their MSC in Information Technology and Management (The Hybrid Manager IGDS Programme). Details of the programme are available from:

IGDS Office
Sheffield Hallam University
School of Computing and Management Sciences
Hallamshire Business Park
100 Napier Street
Sheffield S11 8HD
Telephone (0742) 533109
Fax (0742) 533161

SCALING AND SCORING – IQ

The use of a standard score basis for interpreting intelligence tests – sometimes termed deviation IQ – represents a development some time after the origins of intelligence testing. The term IQ stands for intelligence quotient, originally referring to the ratio or quotient of mental age to chronological age, multiplied by 100. Thus if a child of 11 has a mental age of 11 he is of average mentally and his IQ is 100:

$$\text{here IQ} = 100 \times \frac{\text{Mental Age (11)}}{\text{Chronological Age (11)}}$$

An 11 year old with a mental age of 15 is evidently superior intellectually, while an 11 year old with a mental age of only 7 is inferior intellectually and these differences are reflected in the IQ computed in this way. However, there are difficulties in interpreting IQ in this way as age increases, particularly beyond the age range of normal intellectual development. Thus, a mental age of 11 as opposed to 7 makes sense, in a way that a mental age of 40 versus 30 does not. Thus the deviation IQ provides a more common basis for comparison among intelligence test scores and, indeed, between them and other psychometrics.

STANDARD DEVIATION

The standard deviation of a set of numbers is defined as:

$$\sigma \text{ or SD} = \sqrt{\frac{(\Sigma x^2)}{(N)}}$$

where x represents the individual variations from the mean and N is the number of cases. The square of this viz $\frac{\Sigma x^2}{N}$ is known as the variance. This is not to be confused with the same term used in accountancy to refer to the absolute difference from a budgeted figure.

STANDARD ERROR

The standard error of measurement is given by:

$$\sigma \text{ meas} = \sigma_1 \sqrt{(1 - r_{11})}$$

where σ_1 is the standard deviation scores on a test and r_{11} the reliability coefficient – a correlation between some form of repeat measure of the same test. Note that with perfect reliability the standard error becomes zero.

Bartram (1994) has pointed to the value of considering standard error rather than reliability alone. Among other things he reminds us that a test with the same item repeated over and over would have high reliability, but little practical value.

Appendix 2

Some test publishers and distributors in the UK

ASE
Darville House
2 Oxford Road East
Windsor
Berks
SL4 1DF
Telephone (0753) 850333
Fax (0753) 856830

Oxford Psychologists Press
Lambourne House
311–21 Banbury Road
Oxford
OX2 7JH
Telephone (0865) 510203
Fax (0865) 310368

The Psychological Corporation
Foots Cray High Street
Sidcup
Kent
DA14 5HP
Telephone 081-300 3322
Fax 081-309 0807

Saville and Holdsworth Limited
3 AC Court
High Street
Thames Ditton
Surrey
KT7 0SR

Telephone 081-398 4170
Fax 081-398 9544

Science Research Associates Limited
Newtown Road
Henley-on-Thames
Oxon
RG9 1EW
Telephone (0491) 410111

Appendix 3

Expert system sample report

FULL REPORT ON OCCUPATIONAL PERSONALITY QUESTIONNAIRE

Introduction

Mr Fraser has completed a self-report questionnaire. He also took tests of verbal and numerical critical reasoning.

In the test of verbal critical reasoning, he had to read a number of passages and decide whether several statements logically followed from the information or opinions contained in the passage, whether the opposite followed, or whether it was impossible to tell without further information.

The test of numerical critical reasoning asks questions based on information contained in statistical tables. Here Mr Fraser had to make realistic decisions based on his calculations from these tables, often having to judge whether the information was sufficient to support his decision.

The questionnaire invited him to describe his behaviour, preferences and attitudes, in relation to different aspects of his working life. It is important to recognise that the answers given here are Mr Fraser's own view, and represent the way he sees his behaviour, rather than how his behaviour might be described by another person. This self-report can nevertheless give important clues to understanding Mr Fraser's perception of things and is likely to enable us to predict a good deal about his

---

Copyright Saville & Holdsworth Ltd (1992). The report on this page is the copyright of Saville & Holdsworth Ltd and is reproduced with their kind permission. OPQ is a registered trademark of Saville & Holdsworth Ltd.

behaviour in different situations. The particular version of the questionnaire completed by Mr Fraser required him to make comparative judgements about his behaviour with an element of 'forced choice'. The profile we get from his responses highlights his perceived preferences in typical situations. This report describes Mr Fraser's profile and makes links between the various aspects involved.

Many of the comments made are to a certain extent speculative, and should be understood as hypotheses for further probing or discussion, rather than as definitive pronouncements. His responses to the questionnaire have been compared with those given by a large group of people in professional and managerial jobs.

Relationships with people

He seems to see himself as a leader. He tends to take charge of other people, but he also very much enjoys exercising his powers of persuasion in support of this, to carry others with him. Not only is he thus very influential, but he adds to this by holding rather strong opinions, so that he will come across as a forceful person, even to the extent of being difficult to manage. He has quite a high need for personal autonomy, although he is also reasonably able to develop a sense of identity with the group or organisation, and will not tend to work in too isolated a way.

This marked degree of assertiveness is associated with a reasonable inclination to consult with others, but in a situation of conflict he is likely to make the decisions himself. While he describes himself as having a reasonable sense of the goals towards which influence should be exerted, he might perhaps appear quite a lot more concerned with winning and with achieving a position of power. He will tend to interpret any managerial role quite flexibly, and will supervise people loosely, perhaps failing at times to follow up enough on detail. Not only does he tend to be a very prominent person, but he is also attracted to group situations and his manner of influencing people has a breadth and warmth about it.

Copyright Saville & Holdsworth Ltd (1992). The report on this page is the copyright of Saville & Holdsworth Ltd and is reproduced with their kind permission. OPQ is a registered trademark of Saville & Holdsworth Ltd.

He is quite an outgoing and fun-loving person. He also quite likes being with people, and is likely to be fairly popular. Although he may perhaps not be really interested in developing deeper or intense relationships, he nevertheless likes to behave in a tactful and harmonious way. People are likely to find him quite fun to be with, but perhaps also rather unpredictable, perhaps apt to forget commitments or to disregard some social niceties. He comes across as a socially prominent person. Not only does he seem to be naturally quite sociable, but he has also developed a good deal of confidence and polish to cope well with a range of social situations. He may seem virtually never short of the right phrase to make people feel comfortable. Whilst this social style may usually be perceived as an asset, at times it could seem to be a veneer, or he may flatter others too much for his own good. Positive though his orientation towards people appears, it may also be tinged with a fair degree of self-interest. Thus his relationships could at times seem pragmatic, or his manner a little given to behaving in a political or diplomatic way. Whilst he will probably strike others as having a very high social profile and a commanding presence, he can seem just a little cautious about turning words into action. Mr Fraser has a very high need for recognition of his achievements, and often likes to be in a position to compare favourably with his competitors or colleagues. He rather likes to make his mark but not necessarily according to conventional criteria, and he perhaps even likes to accentuate his separateness from most people. His relative preoccupation with his own status and achievements is further accentuated by what might come across as a lack of interest in the feelings and needs of other people. He may sometimes appear inconsiderate. He may not give people enough opportunity to seek his help, and when they do he may still seem disinterested in the personal difficulties of others. His own relative lack of vulnerability to emotional problems may of course make it very difficult for him fully to empathise with the plight of people in need, or to respond with too much sensitivity to them. Although not seeming to be ready to listen to others or be tolerant of them he can be a keen and

Copyright Saville & Holdsworth Ltd (1992). The report on this page is the copyright of Saville & Holdsworth Ltd and is reproduced with their kind permission. OPQ is a registered trademark of Saville & Holdsworth Ltd.

critical judge of inter-personal issues. While these perceptions may be accurate, his expression of them might appear to lack sympathy at times.

Ability tests

Mr Fraser worked very quickly on the test of verbal critical reasoning, with an average level of accuracy. Although he only worked at an average rate on the test of numerical critical reasoning, he nevertheless made a large number of errors. His ability for evaluating verbal data is assessed as well above average in comparison with the norm group. His response to the handling of numerical data was somewhat less impressive around the average for the same group. He seems relatively more at ease with words, although by no means weak numerically. The facility he showed in the verbal test combined with his high degree of social confidence, would seem to imply an articulate spokesperson. Although reasonably numerate according to his test performance, he showed himself in the questionnaire to have rather little interest in numbers.

Thinking style

Mr Fraser looks to have a predominantly abstract thinking style. His rather adventurous and open mind tends to avoid the structure and discipline needed for a rounded intellectual contribution. His ideas may appear rather broad-brush, and he may need a good deal of administrative support in order to be fully effective. His high overall ability at critical reasoning, as demonstrated in the tests, contrast with a somewhat unstructured approach to problem solving. He may have a more 'natural' mind, which functions better intuitively than methodically. He should have a fair amount of ability at verbal and numerical reasoning tasks, since he is able to translate his reasoning skill into abstract or complex thinking. He is quite

Copyright Saville & Holdsworth Ltd (1992). The report on this page is the copyright of Saville & Holdsworth Ltd and is reproduced with their kind permission. OPQ is a registered trademark of Saville & Holdsworth Ltd.

well attuned to psychology and the people angle of any situation, but may be relatively less comfortable with hard data or numbers. This potential imbalance may make him subjective in his judgement, perhaps prone to over emphasis of human factors beyond the limits implied by cost and other constraints. He has a reasonable interest in visual presentation and in the appreciation of the arts, but seems less concerned about practical aspects, or about understanding how things work.

Mr Fraser likes a fair amount of change and novelty in his life, while his values tend to be middle of the road, neither particularly conservative nor radical. He is quite resilient as well as being moderately adaptable, neither someone who resists change nor one who craves it for its own sake. Although he is reasonably amenable to change, his rather dominant style may make him less open to novel ideas which emanate from others, but still quite an effective change agent himself. Although he is quite interested in theory and intellectual challenge, he rather prefers to avoid the sharp, critical approach which may be needed to ensure a penetrating grasp. He may therefore talk in a general, unfocussed way or take idealistic approaches on board.

His responses suggest a person who is a good generator of ideas and ingenious solutions. Allied to his conceptual approach, this should make him an imaginative innovator. He has a good level of creativity, but he tends to be an ideas person very much more than the solver of everyday practical problems. Given his balanced attitude to change, this degree of creativity may manifest itself more as evolution than revolution, modifications and variations on a theme rather than strokes of genius. His imaginative style is supported by a reasonable degree of purposefulness, so that he should be capable of contributing quite well to strategic discussions. As well as having ideas, he has a great deal of flair in convincing other people of their value. This is allied to a strong will, which can empower his ideas and turn them into policies, but could at times imply strong belief in a somewhat dogmatic approach.

Copyright Saville & Holdsworth Ltd (1992). The report on this page is the copyright of Saville & Holdsworth Ltd and is reproduced with their kind permission. OPQ is a registered trademark of Saville & Holdsworth Ltd.

Mr Fraser seems to believe in a very unstructured method of operating. He does not much like the constraints of pre-determined plans, and he may distinctly prefer to think on his feet. He very much dislikes attentiveness to detail, and tends to find fixed deadlines and bureaucracy irksome. This relatively low interest in planning and preparation may mean that a lot of his marked energy to achieve results will be wasted through pursuit of too many goals, without clear priorities. Although he prefers to work without the constraints of a formal plan, he is less flexible in terms of allowing others to influence the direction of his effort, or to get him to reconsider his priorities.

His definite dislike of detail or routine may be related to his orientation towards the broad perspective. Although he tends to appear disorganised, this may be partly counteracted in terms of his wider view. Not only is he unconcerned with detail, in his approach to problems, but also inclined to be rather unquestioning in his thinking. Not only do his responses suggest a lack of attention to detail, but his test performance confirmed the suspicion that he is basically fairly careless. Not only does he seem to find minutiae very irksome, but also appears distinctly unconcerned about them, and may well be rather inaccurate in his work. Although not very literal in his adherence to schedules, he has a facility for responding to time pressures.

Feelings and emotions

Mr Fraser's responses suggest an effectively dynamic pattern. He combines a very high level of drive and focused concern counter-balanced by a marked self-assurance and control.

He is someone who very rarely experiences anxiety. Not only does he find it easy to switch off from things, but is also able to take even quite severe challenges in his stride. He has a reasonable ability to reduce tension by communicating his own marked freedom from anxiety to others. His distinctly carefree approach also has a rather 'laid-back' character, a relative lack of urgency, about it. His perhaps overly positive and extremely carefree disposition could even make him blind to the possibility of failure.

Copyright Saville & Holdsworth Ltd (1992). The report on this page is the copyright of Saville & Holdsworth Ltd and is reproduced with their kind permission. OPQ is a registered trademark of Saville & Holdsworth Ltd.

He is fairly difficult to upset. He does not easily take offence, and in any case he is likely to be restrained in showing whatever emotions he is experiencing. His marked resilience and low level of tension combine to make him a comfortably adjusted person from an emotional point of view. His strong inner sense of assurance is associated with a considerable amount of interpersonal impact, enabling him to project himself as someone with a very clear self confidence. He seems to be someone who does not have a particularly sensitive disposition. He can put up with a fair amount of rough and tumble, and may be less concerned with matters of feelings.

His attitude to life is very much characterised by optimism and cheerfulness, but at the same time he is reasonably critical and is unlikely to take things too much at face value. His high degree of optimism is linked with a way of seeing things which is more imaginative (sometimes even extravagant) than common place. He has a reasonably communicative brand of cheerfulness, so that his considerable positiveness is fairly visible and can be a source of comfort to others. His fairly cheerful acceptance has an unchallenging, generalised quality, since he is not an attentive listener.

He is someone who sets his sights extremely high, and has a very high determination to succeed against any opposition. He will compete keenly to achieve his aims. Although not attracted to challenges relating to physical endurance *per se*, he sees himself as extremely highly motivated with respect to his career. He tends to see his aspirations in terms of his position or status, but his freedom from anxiety helps him to avoid seeming uptight about them or overly striving. He is likely to behave in a very opportunistic way, seizing chances as they come rather than planning his career in any detail. His ideas of what he wants from his working life may also be less than clear, or perhaps somewhat personal rather than conformist.

He is a person who typically responds quickly and very spontaneously to a situation, perhaps sometimes without enough due reflection. He is capable of making really

Copyright Saville & Holdsworth Ltd (1992). The report on this page is the copyright of Saville & Holdsworth Ltd and is reproduced with their kind permission. OPQ is a registered trademark of Saville & Holdsworth Ltd.

courageous and positive decisions, with little reluctance to work at speed.

He might even lack a due sense of danger on occasion. His decisions are also likely to be clear-cut ones, and carried through with distinct single-mindedness, even against considerable opposition.

Copyright Saville & Holdsworth Ltd (1992). The report on this page is the copyright of Saville & Holdsworth Ltd and is reproduced with their kind permission. OPQ is a registered trademark of Saville & Holdsworth Ltd.

Glossary

Ability test A test in which the ability to perform certain types of task is assessed.

Achievement test A test in which the level acquired in a particular area of skill is assessed (*see also* Attainment test).

Aptitude test A test measuring the aptitude or capacity to master a particular skill area.

Assessment centre An event in which a group of individuals undertake set worklike simulations which are typically assessed by a group of trained assessors who pool their findings before finalising their conclusions.

Attainment test An alternative name for achievement test.

Big five theory of personality A theory which says there are five fundamental aspects of personality, viz extroversion, agreeableness, conscientiousness, neuroticism and intellect.

Brainstorming A method of exploring and developing ideas involving group inputs, initially without discussion or evaluative comment.

Chartered psychologist A person qualified to practise psychology according to the requirements of the British Psychological Society (BPS), as laid down in its Royal Charter and associated statutes, and who is registered with the BPS as chartered and who is bound by a code of professional conduct.

Coaching A process of specific guidance involving giving feedback on performance and advising on methods of improvement.

Cognitive test A test of thinking or mental ability.

Competency An underlying characteristic of an individual, causally related to effective performance.

Concurrent validity The extent to which a test is found to distinguish between two groups, themselves differentiated according to the attribute intended to be measured by the test.

Construct validity The degree to which a test measures the psychological construct or attribute that it is intended to measure.

Content analysis The systematic analysis of the detail of verbal material in either a written or spoken form.

Correlation coefficient A statistic showing the degree of relation between two measures, eg a test score of persistence and sales figures (*see also* Appendix 1).

Counselling A process of helping an individual to understand themselves, their preferences, needs and capabilities through detailed and usually one-to-one discussion.

Cut-off score The level on a test used as a decision point for final or provisional acceptance.

Development centre An assessment centre held particularly for purposes of aiding staff development, often used as an entry point to a development programme.

Direct discrimination Using, race, gender or religion as a criterion for selection or promotion.

Domain mapping A self-analysis technique for an individual to explore the current status of life and work domains relevant to them, and to begin to map a transition path to the desired status.

Face validity The way in which a test appears to be measuring the attribute which it is supposed to measure and/or the degree to which it appears to be a credible process.

Factor An underlying behavioural attribute or characteristic whose existence is established or inferred through factor analysis (*see also* Appendix 1).

Factor analysis A statistical process by which factors are identified through correlational methods (*see also* Appendix 1).

Hybrid manager   A manager able to span between information technology (IT) and its application in business (*see also* Appendix 1).

Indirect discrimination   Using a means of determining selection or promotion decisions which is linked to membership of a particular racial, gender or religious group, rather than ability or potential to perform the job concerned.

Intelligence quotient (IQ)   Originally the ratio of mental age to chronological age. Now used as a generally standardised way of reporting intelligence measures (*see also* Appendix 1).

Interest inventory   A questionnaire comprising items requiring ratings or rankings of preference for different types of task or role or job.

Ipsative   A test item in which comparisons are made between two different attributes, also applied to a test comprising such items.

Item   In a test a question, statement or other stimulus requiring its own separate response.

Multiple regression   The prediction of performance on one variable, such as speed of mastering a software syllabus from scores on a number of other variables, such as scores on the tests in a programmer battery (*see also* Appendix 1).

Negative skew   A condition in which a large number of respondents produce high scores on a test.

Norm   A standard of test scores related to a population or group.

Normal curve   The Gaussian or bell-shaped curve which is applied to the distribution of many attributes (*see also* Appendix 1).

Normative   A term applied to a test item in which a statement is rated directly rather than in comparison with other statements. Also applied to a test made up of such items.

Percentile   The position of a score indicated in relation to the percentage of values in the norm group falling at or below that score.

Personality questionnaire A psychometric instrument, made up of items for self-report designed to reveal typical aspects of behaviour.

Positive skew A condition in which a large number of respondents produce low scores on a test.

Predictive validity The degree to which a test predicts future performance, eg in a job or role or in training.

Selection ratio The proportion of those tested who are selected.

Semantic differential A rating scale in which responses are made in relation to a series of bi-polar statements – eg friendly – reserved.

Standard deviation A statistic describing the spread of scores about a mean value (*see also* Appendix 1).

Standard error The standard deviation of a sampling distribution, used to calibrate the expected variability in a set of scores and so to indicate the range in which the true score might lie (*see also* Appendix 1).

Standardisation The process of producing a set of norms.

Team role A term usually applied to the characteristic behaviours in a team originally described by Meredith Belbin.

Trainability test A test designed to measure the candidates' suitability for undergoing a course of training.

Trait A personality characteristic.

Type A personality description usually based on the work of Carl Gustav Jung.

References

Akin-Ogundeji, O (1991) Asserting Psychology in Africa, *The Psychologist*, v4, pp1–4.

Allnutt, M F (1970) *Performance Under Environmental Stress*, PhD Thesis, University of Nottingham.

American Psychological Association (1954) Technical Recommendations For Psychological Tests And Diagnostic Techniques, *Psychological Bulletin*, v51, 2, Pt 2.

American Psychological Association, American Educational Research Association and National Council on Measurement in Education (1974) *Standards For Educational And Psychological Tests*, American Psychological Association, Washington DC.

Anastasi, A (1961) *Psychological Testing*, The Macmillan Company, New York.

Anstey, E (1977) A 30-Year Follow-up of the CSSB Procedure, with Lessons for the Future, *Journal of Occupational Psychology*, v50, pp149–59.

Argyle, M (1975) *Bodily Communication*, Methuen, London.

Banking Information Service, (1993) *Psychometric Testing: Getting a Better Picture*, Banking Information Service, London.

Bannister, D & Mair J M M (1968) *The Evaluation of Personal Constructs*, Academic Press, London & New York.

Bartram, D (1992) The Personality of UK Managers: 16PF Norms for Short-listed Applicants, *Journal of Occupational Psychology*, v65, pp159–72.

Bartram, D (1994) What Is so Important about Reliability? The Need to Consider the Standard Error of Measurement, *Selection and Development Review*, v10, 1, 1–3.

Belbin, R M (1981) *Management Teams: Why They Succeed or Fail*, Heinemann, London.

Bennett, G K, Seashore, H G & Wesman, A G (1947) *Differential Aptitude Tests*, Psychological Corporation, New York.

Bevan, S & Fryatt, J (1988) *Employee Selection in the UK*, Institute of Manpower Studies, Brighton.

Binet, A & Henri, V (1895) La psychologie individuelle, *Année psychologie*, v2, pp411–63.

Binet, A & Simon, Th (1905) Methodes nouvelles pour le diagnostic du niveau des anormaux, *Année psychologie*, v11, pp191–244.

Bray, D W (1985) Fifty Years of Assessment Centres: A Retrospective and Prospective View, *Journal of Management Development*, v4, no4, pp4–12.

Brindle, L (1992) The Redundant Executive–Typical or Talented, *Selection and Development Review*, v8, no6, pp2–4.

Bryon, M & Modha, S (1991) *How To Master Selection Tests*, Kogan Page, London.

Buros, O (ed) (1941) *The 1940 Mental Measurements Yearbook*, The Mental Measurements Yearbook, New York.

Burt, C (1922) Tests For Clerical Occupations, *JL NIIP*, v1, 23–27, 79–81.

Carr, S & MacLachlan, M (1993) Asserting Psychology in Malawi, *The Psychologist*, v6, no9, pp408–13.

Carroll, J B (1980) *Individual Difference Relations in Psychometric and Experimental Cognitive Tasks*, Report no163, Thurstone Psychometric Laboratory, University of North Carolina, Chapel Hill, NC 27514.

Castle, P F C & Garforth, F I de la P (1951) Selection Training and Status of Supervisors: I Selection, *Occup Psychol*, v25, pp109–123.

Cattell, H B (1989) *The 16PF: Personality In Depth*, Institute For Personality And Ability Testing, Champaign, Illinois.

Cattell, J McK (1890) Mental Tests and Measurement, *Mind*, v15, pp373–80.

Cattell, R B, Eber, H W & Tatsuoka, M (1970) *Handbook For The Sixteen Personality Factor Questionnaire*, Institute For Personality And Ability Testing, Champaign, Illinois.

Cherns, A (1982) Culture and Values: The Reciprocal Influence Between Applied Social Science and its Cultural and Historical Context. In N Nicholson & T D Wall (eds), *The Theory and Practice of Organizational Psychology*, Academic Press, London.

Clark, R & Baron, H (1992) *Guidelines For Testing People With Disabilities*, Saville & Holdsworth Ltd, Thames Ditton.

Clifton, D O & Hall, E (1957) A Projective Technique to Determine Positive and Negative Attitudes Towards People in a Real-Life Situation, *Journal of Educational Psychology*, May, pp273–83.

Clifton, D O & Nelson, P (1992) *Soar With Your Strengths*, Delacorte, New York.

Cook, M (1992) An Evaluation of the DISC/Personal Profile Analysis, *Selection and Development Review*, v8, pp3–6.

Coombs, C H (1964) *A Theory of Data*, Wiley, New York.

Cronbach, L J (1966) *Essentials of Psychological Testing*, 2nd ed, Harper & Row, New York.

Doppelt, J E, Hartman, A D & Krawchik, F B (1984) *Typing Test for Business*, The Psychological Corporation, Sidcup.

Downs, S (1973) *Trainability Assessment-Sewing Machinists*, Industrial Training Research Unit, Cambridge.

Earl, M J (1989) *Management Strategies for Information Technology*, Oxford University Press, Oxford.

Edenborough, R A (1990) Infusing Management with Information Technology, *Atlantic*, April, pp16–17.

Edwards, A L (1959) *Edwards Personal Preference Schedule*, Psychological Corporation, New York.

Evans, W A & Sculli, D (1981) A Comparison of Managerial Traits in Hong Kong and the USA, *Journal of Occupational Psychology*, v54, pp183-6.

Evarts, M (1987) The Competency Programme of the AMA, *Journal of Industrial and Commercial Training*, January/February.

Eysenck, H J (1957) *Sense and Nonsense in Psychology*, Penguin, Harmondsworth.

Feltham, R, Baron, H & Smith, P (1994) Developing Fair Tests, *The Psychologist*, January, pp23-5.

Fletcher, C (1994) Validity, Test Use and Professional Responsibility, *The Psychologist*, January, pp30-1.

Green, B F (1981) A Primer of Testing, *American Psychologist*, v36, pp1001-1011.

Haney, W (1981) Validity, Vaudeville and Values: A Short History of Social Concerns Over Standardized Testing, *American Psychologist*, v36, no10, pp1021-34.

Heneman, H G, Schwab, D P, Huett, D L & Ford, J J (1975) Interview Validity as a Function of Interview Structure, Biographical Data and Interviewee Order, *Journal of Applied Psychology*, v60, pp748-53.

Herriot, P (1987) The Selection Interview. In P B Warr (ed), *Psychology at Work*, Penguin, Harmondsworth.

Hofstede, G (1984) *Culture's Consequences*, Sage, London.

Holt, R R (1958) Clinical and Statistical Prediction: A reformulation and some new data, *Journal of Abnormal and Social Psychology*, v56, pp1-12.

Industrial Relations Services (1994) *Industrial Relations Review and Report, 556*, IRS, London.

Institute of Personnel Management (1993) *IPM Code On Psychological Testing*, IPM, London.

Irvine, S H, Dann, P L & Anderson, J D (1990) Towards a Theory of Algorithm–Determined Cognitive Test Construction, *British Journal of Psychology*, v81, pp173–95.

Jenkins, C D, Zyzanski, J & Roseman, J (1979) Jenkins Activity Survey, The Psychological Corporation, Sidcup.

Johnson, C E, Wood, R & Blinkhorn, S F (1988) Spurioser and Spurioser: The Use of Ipsative Personality Tests, *Journal of Occupational Psychology*, 61, pp153–62.

Jones, J (1987) Utility Analysis in Toplis, J, Dulewicz, V and Fletcher, C *Psychological Testing: A Manager's Guide*, IPM, London.

Kellett, D, Fletcher, S, Callen, A & Geary, B (1994) Fair Testing: The Case of British Rail, *The Psychologist*, January, pp26–9.

Kelly, G A (1955) *The Psychology of Personal Constructs*, v1, Norton, New York.

Krueger, R A (1988) *Focus Groups – A Practical Guide for Applied Research*, Sage, Newbury Park CA.

Krug, S E (1981) *Interpreting 16PF Profile Patterns*, Institute for Personality and Aptitude Testing, Champaign, Illinois.

Latham, G P, Wexley, K N & Pursell, T D (1975) Training Managers to Minimize Rating Errors in Observation of Behaviour, *Journal of Applied Psychology*, v60, pp550–5.

Lee, G & Beard, D (1994) *Development Centres*, McGraw- Hill, London.

Mackenzie Davey, D (1989) *How To Be A Good Judge Of Character*, Kogan Page, London.

Mackinnon, D W (1980) *How Assessment Centres Were Started in the United States: The OSS Assessment Program*, Development Dimensions International, Pittsburgh, USA.

Meyer, H H (1970) The Validity of the In-basket Test as a Measure of Managerial Performance, *Personnel Psychology*, v23, pp297–307.

Morgan, D L (ed) (1993) *Successful Focus Groups*, Sage, Newbury Park CA.

Murray, H A (1938) *Explorations in Personality*, Oxford University Press, New York.

Murray, H A (1943) *Thematic Apperception Test*, Harvard University Press, Cambridge MA.

Myers, C S (1920) Psychology and Industry, *British Journal of Psychology*, 10, pp177–82.

NIIP (1952) The Seven Point Plan, *NIIP Paper No 1*.

NHS Management Executive (1992) *Women in the NHS*, Department of Health, London.

Novick, M R (1981) Federal Guidelines and Professional Standards, *American Psychologist*, v36, no10, pp1035–46.

Osgood, C E (1952) The Nature and Measurement of Meaning, *Psychological Bulletin*, v49, pp197–237.

Palmer, C (1990) 'Hybrids'–A Critical Force in the Application of Information Technology in the Nineties, *Journal of Information Technology*, v5, pp232–5.

Parry, J (1951) The Psychological Adviser's Problems, *Occupational Psychology*, v25, pp124–30.

Prior, D H (1991) *A Perspective on Outplacement: Theory and Current Practice*, MSL Career Consultants, London.

Ridgway, J F (1977) *A Facet Analysis of the Aircrew Film Test*, PhD Thesis, University of Lancaster.

Robertson, I (1994) Personnel Selection Research: Where Are We Now? *The Psychologist*, January, pp17–21.

Rorschach, H C (1942) *Psychodiagnostics: A Diagnostic Test Based on Perception*, Huber, Berne.

Saville, P (1972) *The British Standardisation of the 16PF*, NFER-Nelson Publishing Co Ltd, Windsor, Berks.

Saville, P, Holdsworth, R, Nyfield, G, Cramm, L & Mabey, W (1984) *The Occupational Personality Questionnaires*, SHL, London.

Saville, P & Wilson, E (1991) The Reliability and Validity of Normative and Ipsative Approaches in the Measurement of

Personality, *Journal of Occupational Psychology*, v64, pp219–38.

Schein, E H (1985) Individuals and Careers. In J Lorsch (ed), *Handbook of Organisational Behaviour*, Prentice-Hall, Englewood Cliffs NJ.

Schmidt, F L & Hunter, J E (1977) Development of a General Solution to the Problem of Validity Generalization, *Journal of Applied Psychology*, v62,5, pp529–40.

Schutz, W (1978) *FIRO Awareness Scales Manual*, Consulting Psychologists Press, Palo Alto, California.

Seashore, H & Bennett, G K (1948) *The Seashore-Bennett Stenographic Proficiency Test: A Standard Recorded Stenographic Worksample*, Psychological Corporation, New York.

Shackleton, V & Newell, S (1991) Management Selection: A Comparative Survey of Methods Used in Top British and French Companies, *Journal of Occupational Psychology*, v64, pp23–36.

Smart, D (1983) *Selection Interviewing*, John Wiley & Sons, New York.

Smith, M C & Downs, S (1975) Trainability Assessment for Apprentice Selection in Shipbuilding, *Journal of Occupational Psychology*, v53, pp131–8.

Smith, M, Gregg, M & Andrews, D (1989) *Selection and Assessment, A New Appraisal*, Pitman, London.

Smith, P (ed) (1992) *Motivation and Personality: Handbook of Thematic Content Analysis*, Cambridge University Press, Cambridge.

Spearman, C (1904) General Intelligence, Objectively Determined and Measured, *American Journal of Psychology*, v15, pp201–93.

Spielman, W (1923) Vocational Tests For Dressmakers' Apprentices, *JL NIIP*, 1, pp277–82.

Stott, M B (1950) What Is Occupational Success? *Occup Psychol*, v24, pp105–12.

Stott, M B (1956) Follow Up Problems In Vocational Guidance, Placement and Selection, *Occup Psychol*, v30, pp137–52.

Strong, E K (1943) *Vocational Interests of Men and Women*, Stanford University Press, Stanford CA.

Taylor, H C & Russell, J T (1939) The Relationship of Validity Coefficients to the Practical Effectiveness of Tests in Selection: Discussion and Tables, *Journal of Applied Psychology*, v23, pp565–78.

The Psychological Corporation (1988a) *Assessment for Training and Employment* (ATE), The Psychological Corporation, Sidcup.

Toplis, J, Dulewicz, V and Fletcher, C (1987), *Psychological Testing: A Manager's Guide*, IPM, London.

Vincent, D F (1955) Speed and Precision in Manual Skill, *NIIP Report*, no11.

Vincent, D F (1971) Problems of Test Production and Supply, *Occupational Psychology*, v44, pp71–80.

Watson, G & Glaser, E M (1991) *Critical Thinking Appraisal Manual*, The Psychological Corporation, Sidcup.

Wechsler, D (1955) *Wechsler Adult Intelligence Scale*, Psychological Corporation, New York.

Williams, R S (1994) Occupational Testing: Contemporary British Practice, *The Psychologist*, January, pp11–13.

Yoakum, C & Yerkes, R M (1920) *Army Mental Tests*, Holt, New York.

Index